CANADA AND NATIONAL MISSILE DEFENCE

The Canadian Institute of Strategic Studies

Chairman of the Board of Directors: Jean Jacques Blais, QC, PC, BA, LLB
President: Alex Morrison, MSC, CD, MA
Executive Director: David Rudd, MA
Associate Executive Director: Jim Hanson, CD, Eng Cert, MA, CET
Research Officer: Jessica Blitt, MA

The Canadian Institute of Strategic Studies provides the forum for, and is the vehicle to stimulate, the research, study, analysis, and discussion of the strategic implications of major national and international issues, events, and trends as they affect Canada and Canadians

The CISS is currently working independently or in conjunction with other organizations in a variety of fields, including international peacekeeping; Canadian security and sovereignty; arms control and disarmament; Canada-US security cooperation; and regional security studies.

CISS PUBLICATIONS INCLUDE:

FREE WITH MEMBERSHIP:
- Spring/Fall Seminar Proceedings
- Strategic Datalinks
- Strategic Profile: Canada
- The CISS Bulletin
- Canadian Military Journal/Revue Canadienne Militaire
- Peacekeeping and International Relations

BY SUBSCRIPTION:
- The McNaughton Papers

The CISS is an independent, non-profit organization. For membership, seminar, and publications information contact:

The Canadian Institute of Strategic Studies
2300 Yonge Street, Suite 402, Box 2321
Toronto, Ontario, M4P 1E4
Tel: (416) 322-8128; Fax: (416) 322-8129
E-mail: info@ciss.ca
Http://www.ciss.ca

CISS Annual Spring Seminar 2000

CANADA AND NATIONAL MISSILE DEFENCE

Edited by

David Rudd
Jim Hanson
Jessica Blitt

The Canadian Institute of Strategic Studies

The Canadian Institute of Strategic Studies
Copyright 2000

The Canadian Institute of Strategic Studies meets a need for a body of information on Canadian security issues and it promotes public awareness of the significance of national and international developments. The CISS provides a forum for discussion of strategic matters and, through its educational and informational activities, it seeks to improve the basis for informed choice by the Canadian public.

Canadian Cataloguing in Publication Data

Main entry under title:

Canada and national missile defence

Proceedings of the CISS annual spring seminar, held in Ottawa, Apr. 20, 2000.
Includes bibliographical references.
ISBN 0-919769-94-2

1. Ballistic missile defenses - Canada - Congresses. 2. Canada – Military relations - United States - Congresses. 3. United States - Military relations - Canada - Congresses. 4. Ballistic missile defenses - Congresses. I. Rudd, David. II. Hanson, Jim, 1938- . III. Blitt, Jessica, 1974- . IV. Canadian Institute of Strategic Studies. Spring Seminar (2000 : Ottawa, Ont.).

UG745.C3C36 2000   358.1'74'0971   C00-932124-1

The CISS acknowledges the assistance of Lisa Ann Bokwa and Tyler Cummings during the seminar. The Institute would also like to thank John Fairley for his assistance in preparing the proceedings.

TABLE OF CONTENTS

Glossary..vii

Introduction
David Rudd..1

Opening Remarks
David Pratt, MP..5

The US-Proposed National Missile Defence System: The East Asian Response
Dr. Robert D'A. Henderson..7

The European Dimension of Ballistic Missile Defence
Dr. Jim Fergusson..27

Factors Affecting Canada's Approach to National Missile Defence
The Honourable Art Eggleton...39

Minister's Forum...45

Morning Forum 49

The Case Against National Missile Defence: A Canadian Perspective
Bill Robinson..57

Canada and National Missile Defence: A NORAD Perspective
LGen (Retd) Robert W. Morton..69

National Missile Defence and the Future of Canada-US Defence Cooperation
Dr. Joseph T. Jockel...83

Afternoon Forum..91

Closing Remarks
BGen (Retd) W. Don Macnamara..103

GLOSSARY

ABM	Anti-Ballistic Missile
ACCS	air command and control system
APAR	active planar array radar
AWACS	Airborne Warning and Control System
BMD	ballistic missile defence
BMDO	Ballistic Missile Defense Organization
BMEWS	Ballistic Missile Early Warning System
C2	command and control
C4I	Command, Control, Communications, Computers, Intelligence
CIA	Central Intelligence Agency
CONUS	Continental United States
CTBT	Comprehensive Test Ban Treaty
DCI	Defence Capabilities Initiative
DCINC	Deputy Commander-in-Chief (NORAD)
DEW	Distant Early Warning
DFAIT	Department of Foreign Affairs and International Trade
DIA	Defense Intelligence Agency
DND	Department of National Defence (Canada)
DPP	Democratic Progressive Party
DSP	Defense Support Program
EAD	Extended Air Defence
EIAD	Extended Integrated Air Defence
ESDI	European Security and Defence Identity
FOLs	Forward Operating Locations
INF	Intermediate Nuclear Forces
ITARs	International Trade in Arms Regulations
ITWAA	Integrated Tactical Warning and Attack Assessment
JDA	Japanese Defense Agency
KMT	Kuomintang Party (Taiwan)
MAD	Mutually Assured Destruction
MEADS	medium extended air defence system
MIRV	multiple independent reentry vehicle
MoU	Memorandum of Understanding
MTCR	Missile Technology Control Regime
NAC	North Atlantic Council
NATINADS	NATO Integrated Air Defence System
NATO	North Atlantic Treaty Organization
NDOC	National Defence Operations Centre
NMCC	National Military Command Centre, Washington

NMD	National Missile Defence
NORAD	North American Aerospace Defence
NPT	Non-Proliferation Treaty
NTW	Navy Theatre-Wide
NWS	North Warning System
PAAMS	principal anti-air missile system
PAC	Patriot Advanced Capability
R&D	research and development
RCC	Regional Command Centre
ROK	Republic of Korea
SDI	Strategic Defense Initiative
SDIO	Strategic Defense Initiative Organization
SHAPE	Supreme Headquarters Allied Powers Europe
SLBM	submarine-launched ballistic missile
SRBM	short-range ballistic missile
START	Strategic Arms Reduction Treaty
THAAD	Theater High Altitude Area Defence
TMD	theatre missile defence
UN	United Nations
WMD	weapons of mass destruction

INTRODUCTION

David Rudd

Ladies and gentlemen, good morning and a warm welcome to the annual spring seminar of the Canadian Institute of Strategic Studies. This marks the first time in six years that the Institute has held one of its two semi-annual seminars in Ottawa. Our intention in doing so is twofold: first, it is to give our members living in the Ottawa area a chance to participate in CISS activities; secondly, it is to facilitate discussion and debate among opinion- and policy-makers here in the nation's capital.

The topic is Canada and National Missile Defence (NMD). Although public debate on the issue has been sporadic, it has also been rather passionate, with strongly held views expressed on the airwaves and on the editorial pages of major newspapers. The arguments with which we are familiar have dealt with only a few aspects of missile defence, and the implications of Canada's participation or non-participation in the US program remain largely speculative. There has been little direct interaction between the partisans in this debate, and in the end the majority of the attentive public is left wondering what NMD is all about, what is at stake for Canadians, and what constitutes wise policy in this case. This is a difficult issue to examine, let alone summarize for public consumption. So in the battle for public opinion, the opinion-makers must realize that they bear enormous responsibility for their policy prescriptions. There is potentially much to be gained and much to be lost, regardless of how this issue is decided in Canada.

We know that National Missile Defence has its roots in American concerns over the proliferation of missile technology to less than stable parts of the world. (The simultaneous proliferation of weapons of mass destruction — nuclear, biological and chemical — have heightened these

---

David Rudd is Executive Director of the CISS.

concerns). We also know that NMD is different in content and scope from the politically and technologically discredited Strategic Defence Initiative (SDI) of the 1980s. Whereas the latter envisioned a space-based suite of weapons and sensors providing the US with protection form a massive Soviet missile attack, NMD is intended to offer protection from a limited attack from smaller countries.

What we do not yet know is how the proposed system will affect relations between states. There is speculation that the deployment of the system will result in the abandonment of arms control regimes that have constrained the growth of nuclear arsenals. Others counter that NMD is strictly defensive, that it poses no threat to anyone, and that it provides a degree of protection that arms control cannot. Mixed in with the political dimension is the technical feasibility of the system. Does the test program set a realistic pace for research and development? Will multi-spectral sensors allow NMD to distinguish between incoming warheads and decoys? Or is the entire concept a latter-day version of the infamous Maginot Line — a technological marvel that can nevertheless be circumvented by an opponent?

Our approach today is perhaps a bit unorthodox. We have decided to set the stage for a discussion on Canada and NMD by first examining some of the important regional viewpoints on ballistic missile defence. We shall spend the better part of the morning reviewing some of the opinions of key states who feel that they have a stake in the US program. This afternoon we shall move on to an examination of what Canada's options are with regard to NMD and what the results of those policy decisions might be.

Ladies and gentlemen, we are here not only to enhance your understanding of the topic, but to provide you with an academic setting in which to topic can be discussed. We believe that this is important because issues involving Canada-US defence relations in general, and issues involving strategic matters in particular, are often treated as political footballs to be kicked around and accompanied by a generous amount of intemperate language and rhetoric. Regrettably, it is often the case in public policy debates that ideas are ridiculed instead of rebutted. So we invite you to carefully consider the statements and assumptions made by our speakers before you challenge them. But challenge them you must.

We will not always agree on what constitutes good policy, but whatever policy orientation emerges from the current debate, Canadians have the right to expect that policy will be the result of prudent and purposeful choice. Our policy on NMD cannot be left to drift or to be made by default or on an *ad hoc* basis. We cannot be sure if our assessments of the effect NMD on either Canada-US relations or broader international relations will be accurate. A certain degree of imprecision will have to be expected. So let us open our minds and proceed cautiously. The stakes are too high to do otherwise.

Before we begin, I would like to thank our speakers and moderators for their hard work in preparing for and leading the seminar. I would also like to recognize Associate Executive Director Jim Hanson for organizing the event, and Research Officer Jessica Blitt and her team of volunteers for seeing to the administrative duties this morning. I'd also like to thank the staff here at the University of Ottawa for providing a venue for today's proceedings. Lastly, I would like to thank all of you, the members of our "studio audience", for coming today. We hope that you will enhance our seminar by lending your curiosity and insights to the question-and-answer sessions.

OPENING REMARKS

David Pratt, MP

I'd like to thank David Rudd for inviting me to participate in this seminar. It's a pleasure for me to be here to introduce our speakers for this morning. The subject of National Missile Defence is indeed a weighty one. The Standing Committee on National Defence and Veterans Affairs, of which I am Vice-Chair, has heard a number of speakers on the subject over the last couple of months. I expect we are going to hear a few more in the months to come. To say that it is a weighty topic is a bit of an understatement. It has, as I'm sure all of you would agree, some very wide-ranging implications for international relations in general, as well as defence policy, weapons technology, and the whole issue of non-proliferation. It raises particularly interesting questions for Canada in terms of its possible or potential participation. What are the implications, for instance, for NORAD if we refuse to participate? Also, do we accept the US argument about the legitimacy of the current and potential threats? Does the US have the right to defend itself against a real or perceived threat irrespective of what it might do to existing arms control agreements? Other questions, I think, are raised as well, in terms of the ABM treaty. After over 25 years, is it in fact obsolete? And what happens to the whole concept of mutually assured destruction?

So, with that very brief introduction, let us get to the business at hand.

David Pratt is Member of Parliament for Nepean-Carleton and Vice-Chair of the Standing Committee on National Defence and Veterans Affairs (SCONDVA).

THE US- PROPOSED NATIONAL MISSILE DEFENCE SYSTEM: THE EAST ASIAN RESPONSE

Dr. Robert D'A. Henderson

The Missile Firing Heard Across the Pacific

On 31 August 1998 the North Korean communist regime of Kim Jong Il test launched a three-stage Taepo Dong 1 long-range ballistic missile from its test site on the Sea of Japan. The three-stage missile dropped its first stage in the Sea of Japan and then passed over the northern Japanese island of Hokkaido with the second stage splashing down in the Northwest Pacific and the third stage apparently going into orbit. With an estimated range of 2000 km (1250 miles) this missile test proved that North Korea had the missile capable to hit any point in Japan and quite likely reach western Alaska and perhaps even the Hawaiian Islands (See Figure 1). This was a considerable technological advance on North Korea's 1993 test launch of its medium-range Nodong missile — an enhanced two-stage Soviet Scud "clone" with an estimated range of 450 km (300 miles).

While American leaders in Washington D.C. apparently had some advance warning of the 1998 North Korean test preparations, the Taepo Dong 1 launch was a surprise to Japan's national leaders. They were shocked by the fact that the North Korean missile had flown over Hokkaido, one of their main islands. In the media, Japanese commentators openly questioned whether the United States had been derelict in its sharing of defence intelligence with Japan by not providing advance information to Tokyo on the missile launch. Even in Washington, there was serious concern about the unexpected advances in North Korea's missile development program — especially in view of the longer range of the Taepo Dong 1 missile and its evident capacity to place a "warhead" in orbit or bring it down on a distant target.

Dr. Robert D'A. Henderson is Senior Strategic Analyst, Global Affairs, R+E+A Group, Ottawa.

Figure 1

Theater Missile Defense and North Korean offensive capacity

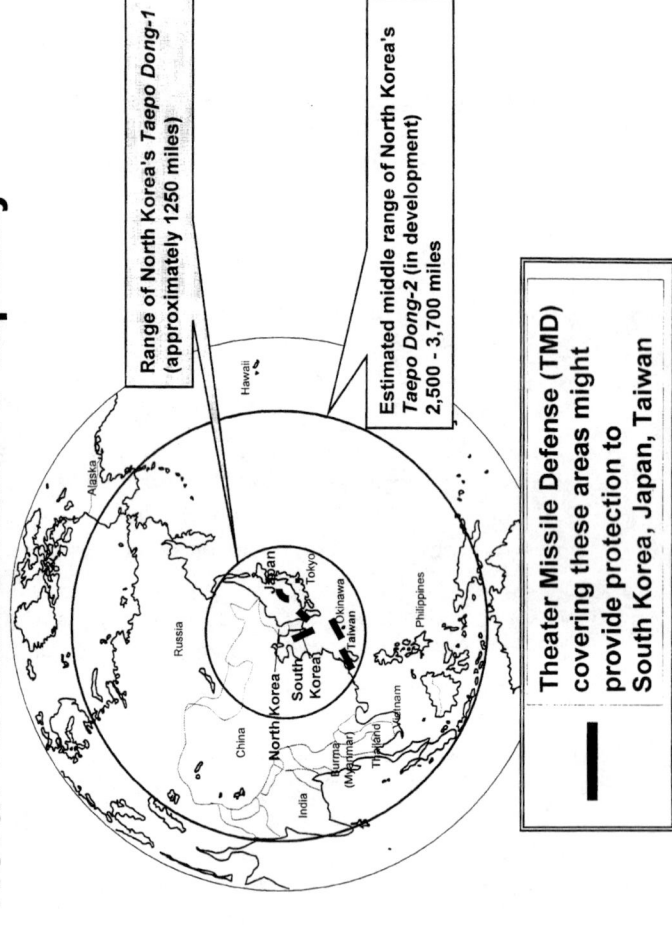

The United States has repeatedly pointed to the threat from "rogue states" — such as North Korea, Iran, Iraq and Libya — and "others" acquiring a ballistic missile capability. The Central Intelligence Agency (CIA) and the Defense Intelligence Agency (DIA) have warned of the growing threat of ballistic missiles which could carry weapons of mass destruction (WMD) over the next five to fifteen years — agreeing that North Korea constitutes the major threat in the short term.[1] Following the National Missile Defense Act being signed into law by President Bill Clinton in 1999, Secretary of Defense William Cohen visited South Korea and Japan to discuss the North Korean missile threat and the prospects for the formation of regional ballistic missile defences in East Asia — though he received different responses from Seoul and Tokyo.[2]

The "Star Wars" Legacy

In March 1983, US President Ronald Reagan announced his Strategic Defense Initiative (SDI) proposal for a defensive umbrella of satellite detection systems and space-based futuristic technologies — such as lasers, particle beams, interceptor missiles, etc. — to destroy intercontinental ballistic missiles in ascent and mid-flight. His initial "Star Wars" vision was quickly revised into a "Star Wars II" proposal to make it more acceptable politically to domestic constituencies and legally in terms of international agreements. A research funding "carrot" was held out to allied governments for their participation in SDI technology research, but ultimately almost all of the SDI research funding was awarded to American concerns along with the prospective commercial technology benefits. The US government funded these prospective technologies through its Strategic Defense Initiative Organization (SDIO), renamed the Ballistic Missile Defense Organization (BMDO) in 1993. In any case, the necessary technology for detection, communications and interdiction was years — if not decades — away from being developed and deployed and at an enormous cost in research funding. This "Star Wars II" research in its turn lead to a "Star War Jr." research effort to develop a more limited regional missile defence capacity to protect Western Europe, Israel, or Japan.[3]

With the collapse of the communist regimes in Eastern Europe and the Soviet Union, there was a decrease in domestic pressure within the United States for the development of the necessary technology to deploy a workable anti-ballistic missile system over North America. This domestic pressure rose again with the 1991 Gulf War when Iraqi forces under Saddam Hussein launched medium-range Soviet-built Scud missiles into Saudi Arabia, where American and allied forces were deployed, and into

Israel. This missile threat to US troops overseas strengthened the calls for developing a theater missile defence (TMD) system. Throughout the early 1990s, Western intelligence services warned of the increasing threat of ballistic missiles from so-called "rogue states." Pressure increased for the deployment of a workable TMD — a "Star Wars Jr." — against short-range missiles like the Soviet-built Scud, as the anti-missile technologies were less ambitious and more likely to work. But anti-missiles interceptors, like the Patriot anti-missile missile, only operate against incoming missiles in their terminal phase and therefore protect a small area. What was required for a TMD system was space-based satellites to detect the missile launch, enhanced missiles to intercept and destroy the incoming missiles either within the atmosphere or as they approach their target area, and the computer capacity to control the interdiction process. The NATO aerial offensive in the former Yugoslavia and Kosovo established that the United States had the capacity to operate very complex communications technology warfare in real time — a direct legacy of its years of research and billions of dollars invested in "Star War" computer technology.[4]

North Korea's 1993 successful test of its extended-range Nodong missile confirmed that the 37,000 American troops stationed in South Korea were vulnerable to missile strikes — as well as in other regions where American forces were deployed and where North Korea had clandestinely sold missiles. Following the 1993 Nodong missile launch, the United States renewed its "quiet discussions" with its East Asian allies — particularly Japan — for their participation in developing and deploying a TMD system in the region. In the United States, the North Korean missile test heated up the "anti-missile defence" debate, highlighting the need for a "basic" [ie. limited] missile defence system for North America. Not surprisingly, the issues in the "Star War" debate of the late 1980s began all over again with calls for a limited national missile defense to cover North America and a "Star Wars Jr." theater missile defence for American armed forces based overseas — particularly in the East Asian region. China's 1996 missile launches near Taiwan (in an attempt to deter Taiwanese voters during their first democratic presidential elections[5]) only reinforced the American government's determination to develop the necessary anti-missile technology.

The East Asian Responses

Japan's Response

In 1987, as one of the "invited" allied governments, Japan signed an SDI co-operative agreement with the United States regarding technology research and commercial rights. But American proposals from 1993 on for Japanese participation in developing a workable missile defence were met with Japanese government disinterest or coalition government objections. This disinterest changed following the August 1998 North Korean missile test over the country — a result of which was increased public support for missile defences and domestic reconnaissance satellites.[6] In November of that year, the Japanese cabinet approved the development of its own reconnaissance satellite capability with funding for four satellites, the first to be launched in 2002. Interestingly, South Korea — with all of its territory within range of operational North Korean missiles — noted that Japan's planned satellite system could change the regional security situation, possibly leading to heightening tensions.[7]

In the debate on whether Japan should develop missile defences, there was the question as to whether such defences could be a violation of the country's post-war "peace" constitution — namely Article 9 which prohibits Japan from possessing offensive weapons. The Government position was set out in its *White Paper on Defence 1999*, which pointed out that "North Korea's missile development concerns not just Asia but the international community as a whole" and went on to call for increased co-operation between the United States and Japan on defense against ballistic missiles. According to Nobumasa Ohta, Japanese Defense Agency (JDA) spokesman, "We [Japan] can exercise our right to defense against enemy facilities once it's confirmed that the enemy has embarked on an action to attack us ... Striking back in not unconstitutional." In effect, a strike against foreign bases from which missiles were aimed at Japan would *not* be a violation of Article 9.[8]

In August 1999, the US Department of Defense and the Japanese Defense Agency signed a memorandum of understanding (MoU) detailing the contents of the joint research and development for the TMD system, as well as clearly stating that the two sides would share the technology and information obtained in the process of research and who retains commercial rights to the research results. Based on shared research funding, the five-year program is expected to concentrate on enhancements to the US Navy's Standard SM-3 interceptor missile for use with the Navy Theater-Wide (NTW) missile defence program. This will be done by research linkages between American and Japanese companies, such as the link between Raytheon Corporation and Mitsubishi Heavy Industries Ltd. on a new generation of SM-3 missile. The upgraded SM-3 would be deployed on the four Aegis battle management destroyers which Japan already operates. The Aegis radar and computer array is capable of tracking more than 100 targets on land, air and sea simultaneously (See Figure 2).

Figure 2

Ship and land-based theater missile defence protection against North Korean *Taepo Dong-1* missiles

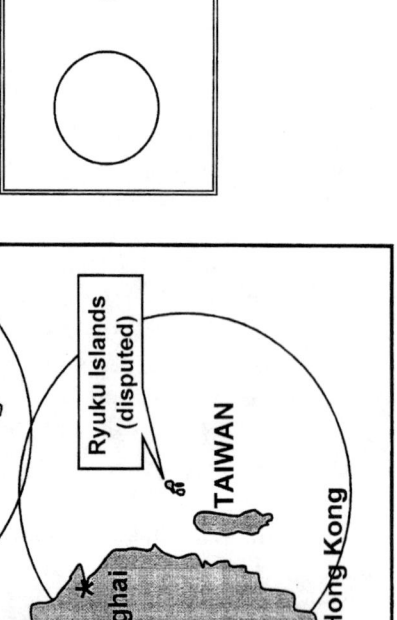

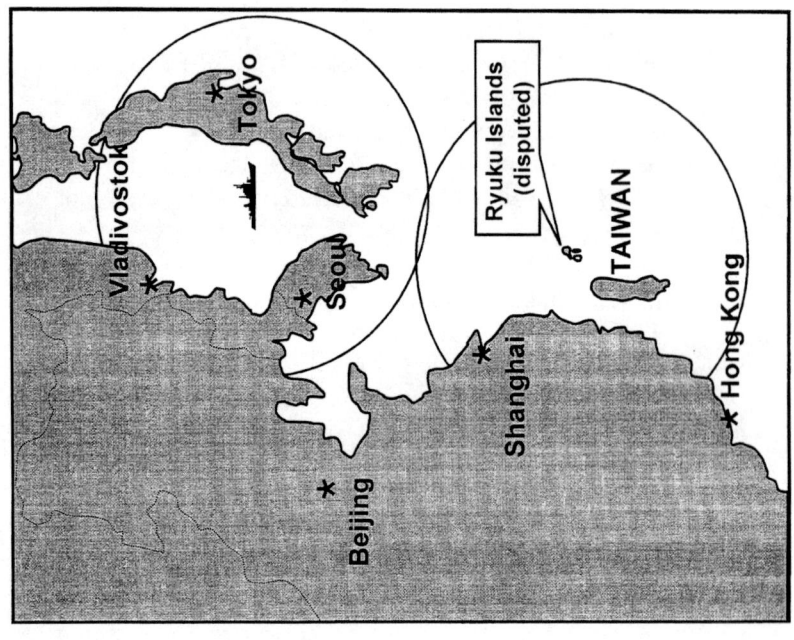

This would provide the "operational base" for the Japanese Defence Agency to deploy a mobile intercept capability close to suspect missile launch sites, such as the North Korean test site near Rodong along its eastern coast facing the Sea of Japan, or even the Chinese missile bases in the coastal provinces along the East China Sea.

But the Japanese government has maintained that it will only decide whether to proceed beyond the research stage after studying the technological feasibility of the program. At this time, the Japanese government has not made any decision on moving from anti-missile research development to missile defence production and deployment and it is unlikely to do so until after the joint feasibility research is completed. Such an decision would require a second MoU regarding funding for the anti-missile deployment and space-based satellite monitoring necessary for a sea-based NTW system with a possible deployment sometime by 2010. This is the option preferred by the JDA. The NTW system would require less new equipment than other missile defence options such as the land-based Theater High Altitude Area Defence (THAAD) system which is also under development in the United States. Reportedly, a Japanese Aegis destroyer tracked the Taepo Dong 1 test-firing in 1998 from its launch in North Korea to its impact northeast of Hokkaido — though the ship had no capacity to "shoot" it down if it had been aimed at a Japanese homeland target. The projected NTW system — based on Japanese Aegis destroyers operating in the Sea of Japan and the East China Sea or even restricted to Japanese territorial waters — should be able to provide missile protection over all the main islands of Japan as well as most of the airspace from the Russian Maritime Region (around Vladivostok) in the North to the island of Taiwan in the South.[9]

The Japanese government has approved funding for the development of national reconnaissance satellites, with the first to be launched by 2002. In addition to the Taepo Dong missile launch, the cabinet decision apparently was based on the view that Japan would continue to lag behind the United States "forever" unless it tried to develop satellites "on its own."[10] Until the Japanese national satellites are operational, the JDA will continue to be reliant upon American defence intelligence-sharing. Only in early 1996 did the US Defense Department agree to supply the JDA with downlinks for receiving early warning satellite intelligence on regional missile launches, despite the JDA's standing request for this intelligence, which dated back to North Korea's 1993 test launch.[11] But, to reduce its dependence on US defence intelligence, the JDA has also begun to purchase "spy satellite" quality imagery from the American private sector. Space Imaging Inc.'s Ikonos high-resolution satellite has the imaging technology to distinguish an object as small as 82 centimetres wide on the ground. The JDA will also purchase a ground station and an image information support system to receive and analyse the Ikonos photographic data.[12]

South Korea's Response

Unlike Japan, the 1998 launch of North Korea's Taepo Dong 1 produced little response from South Korea. This was largely due to the fact that the entire southern portion of the Korean Peninsula was already within range of North Korean medium-range missiles. In fact, the capital Seoul is within range of tactical battlefield rockets and long-range artillery from the North Korean side of the demilitarized zone (DMZ). But it could also have been due to the policy of engagement with the authoritarian North Korean regime being pursued by the government of President Kim Dae-jung since it took office in February 1998. This so-called "Sunshine Policy" is an attempt to develop normal relations with Pyongyang and reduce tensions on the Korean Peninsula.

When approached by the US in the early 1990s to participate in a proposed regional TMD system, Republic of Korea (ROK) leaders apparently showed little interest, preferring to get American agreement for its internal development of a medium-range missile which could reach even the northernmost part of North Korea. But South Korea has a 20-year agreement with the United States which restricts its missiles to a range of not more than 180 km (110 miles). South Korea has been demanding the right — and the US technology — to build missiles with a range of 500 km (310 miles), enough to reach any part of North Korea.

On the issue of TMD, Seoul has maintained that such a regional missile defence system could generate controversy among its militarily stronger neighbours — including China and Russia which oppose it and Japan and Taiwan which are generally supportive of such defences — and that it could lead to an arms race in Northeast Asia. In March 1999, South Korean Defence Minister Choon Yong-taek stated that the proposed TMD was "not an effective measure to counter Pyongyang's missile threats in consideration of Seoul's finances and technology." In fact, Seoul is almost completely defenceless against an attack by North Korean short-range missiles and even long-range artillery. The South Korean government reaffirmed this position a couple months later in the face of reported American pressure for it to reconsider.[13] But following

Defense Secretary Cohen's July visit, there appeared to be US-South Korean agreement on two points. First, that the United States would sell additional Patriot anti-missile batteries to South Korea, including 14 of the latest Patriots upgraded to Patriot Advanced Capability 3 (PAC-3) standard. Second, that the United States would reconsider the range restrictions on South Korea's own indigenous missile force, up to a range of 500 km.[14] Even when the new PAC-3 missiles are deployed, much of the South Korean population, as well as most of the ROK military facilities, will still lack an anti-missile "umbrella".[15]

North Korea's Response

Although it is the offensive threat of its own missile force which has lead to renewed pressure by the United States for a regional TMD in East Asia, the authoritarian regime in Pyongyang has constantly denounced the American-proposed TMD system as a direct threat to its own national sovereignty. The regime of the "Dear Leader" Kim Jong Il sees such a TMD system as a shield behind which South Korea and the United States — with its 37,000 troops stationed in South Korea — could attack the North without fear of retaliation by North Korea's Nodong missiles. Diplomatically, creating a TMD system will reduce North Korea's so-called "missile leverage" in its talks with the United States and Japan for foreign assistance — including money, oil, and food supplies. This partly accounts for the North's denouncements of Japan for "getting more zealous" in its joint TMD research with the United States.[16] Repeatedly, North Korean government spokesmen have warned that Pyongyang would counter such a US-dominated missile defence system by an "increase its [own] arms build-up" — most likely a reference to an increase in its medium-range missile production. But there are questions as to whether North Korea has the resources to increase its missile production for domestic purposes, particularly as it is understood that it gets the majority of its foreign exchange from the clandestine sale of these medium-range missiles to other countries.[17]

In September of 1999, North Korea reportedly agreed to forgo what appeared to be preparations for a test of its newly-developed longer-range Taepo Dong 2 missile in return for the lifting of some economic sanctions by the United States. According to recent CIA intelligence estimates on the North Korean ballistic missile threat, the three-stage Taepo Dong 2 will be capable of delivering a large nuclear warhead anywhere in the continental United States. While Pyongyang is thought to have continued its long-range missile development research, it has not test-fired such missiles while the bilateral talks with the United States were under way. Meanwhile, despite some progress in the United States-North Korea missile talks in Berlin, the US and Japan have agreed to continue with their TMD research.[18]

Taiwan's Response

Following the 1996 Chinese missile tests off Taiwan's northern and southern ports, the KMT government under President Lee Teng-hui purchased PAC-2 missile batteries from the United States for deployment around the capital Taipei. When the Clinton Administration proposed a joint TMD system for the East Asian region, the KMT government badly wanted to join and stated so publicly. But due to the United States' "One China" policy and the Clinton Administration's need to keep the Beijing government "constructively engaged" in bilateral relations, the Taiwan request was quietly rebuffed by Washington. In response, then-Defence Minister Tang Fei publicly stated that Taiwan had really meant that it would develop its own "national" low-altitude terminal missile defence and had not ask to participate in the proposed high-altitude TMD system. He went on to point out that Taiwan was beginning to work on development of its own anti-missile missiles.[19]

While it develops its own anti-missile technology, Taiwan will continue to depend upon the United States for its limited missile defences. In July 1999, President Lee referred to Taiwan-China relations as "state-to-state" with suggestions of independence for Taiwan. This resulted in heightened tensions with China and fears of renewed Chinese missile launches toward the island.[20] Taipei was forced to ask the United States to sell it three upgraded PAC-3 systems for deployment around Taipei, even though these anti-missiles can only cover a small area. Then, in early 2000, the KMT government announced that it was requesting an additional three PAC-3 systems for deployment in central Taiwan near its high tech industries and near the southern port of Kaohsiung where the island's petroleum storage reserves are located.

Under the 1979 Taiwan Security Act, the United States is committed to providing such defensive armaments to Taiwan to ensure its security. In Taiwan's annual weapons request this year, the KMT Government had asked to purchase four Aegis destroyers as the basis of its own TMD system. The request was turned down, although it "could be considered in another year." Washington did agree to sell Taiwan a long-range Pave Paw radar system which is capable of "looking" deep into China, greatly enhancing the island's early warning capability. When installed, the Pave Paw radar could become a key component in a future TMD system for the island. Nevertheless, a NTW missile defence system operated from either US or Japanese Aegis destroyers deployed to the north of Taiwan could be able to provide a defensive "footprint" over the entire island. China has already noted that the deployment of a TMD system "at the two edges of the Ryukyu Islands will play the same role as the deployment of the weapon system to Taiwan in a military sense."[21]

Even though the opposition Democratic Progressive Party (DPP) candidate Chen Shui-bian defeated the ruling KMT candidate Lien Chan in the March 18, 2000 presidential elections, it appears that the new Taiwan government will continue to favour joining an American TMD system if asked. Chen Shui-bian declared last November that he favoured Taiwan joining the US-proposed missile defences. Similarly, in December, a DPP China Affairs study group concluded in its first special report on the proposed TMD that there was a "national" need for such a missile defence system for Taiwan and that Taiwan should strive for technology transfer in the purchase of such TMD hardware.[22] In April President Clinton deferred a decision on selling four Aegis-equipped destroyers — as well as enhanced PAC-3 missiles and P-3 Orion anti-submarine aircraft — to Taiwan. Noting that the sale of Aegis destroyers was "not cancelled but deferred," president-elect Chen Shui-bian went on to state that "if China can prevent [Taiwan's] missile deployment and issue military threats, there will be no TMD by the United States and even if [Taiwan] wants to there would be no TMD to join."[23] Nevertheless, there have been news reports that an "unidentified client" (thought to be Taiwan) contracted Space Imaging Inc. for its Ikonos satellite to take a series of high resolution images of the mainland's eastern region. It is thought that the satellite took images of seven target areas, including Chinese missile and aircraft bases facing Taiwan, over three dates in February, March and April of this year.[24] While the United States will likely provide Taiwan with satellite intelligence in the event of a military conflict with China, such high-resolution Ikonos photographs will permit the island's defence planners to gage Chinese military preparations during times of tension.

In December 1999, the KMT government called for Taiwan to develop a long-range surface-to-surface missile deterrent to counter China's missiles. Speaking at a Taiwan security forum, Vice-President Lien Chan stated that "in order to deter the enemy [China] from invading Taiwan, we have to develop a reliable deterrent and beef up the second-strike capability." However, the next day Defence Minister Tang Fei described

Vice-President Lien Chan's comments regarding the development of long-range missiles as an "official viewpoint" but not "official policy". There was apparent concern that declaring a government intention to develop an enhanced second-strike capability would be seen by China as a complement to the future deployment of a regional TMD and part of a government plan to declare Taiwan independent from the mainland.[25]

China's Response

From the beginning, China has consistently and vocally opposed the American plans for creating a National Missile Defense (NMD) system — to which it refers as Washington's "Sky Net Dream." China's position has been that, though a defensive technology in name, the anti-missile technology being developed by the United States enables it to attack its enemies while defending itself. Once deployed, a NMD or TMD could help the United States to contain the offensive ballistic missile forces that an enemy state could bring into play. According to Sha Zukang, director of the Arms Control Department in the Chinese Foreign Ministry, "China does not reject the whole concept of theater missile defense (TMD). Although China understands the value of TMD in protecting stationed troops, it opposes advanced TMD systems that could be used in National Missile Defenses (NMD)...in space and elsewhere."[26] A TMD system deployed within East Asia could be used to protect Taiwan from being reintegrated into mainland China (See Figure 2) — an overriding priority for the communist leadership in Beijing, particularly since Hong Kong and Macao have now rejoined China.[27] Communist leaders in Beijing fear that, even if Taiwan is not invited to join the regional TMD or sold the necessary hardware and technology, the joint US-Japanese missile defence research will lead to implementing a working TMD which could in practice be used to cover Taiwan as well as American, and possibly Japanese, naval forces intervening to protect the island. According to Vice-Premier Qian Qichen, "We [China] firmly oppose the sale by foreign forces of advanced weapons to Taiwan or the sale or transfer of technology related to the so-called theater missile defense system."[28] Ironically, China, like North Korea, has been accused of selling missile technology to US-designated "rogue states" such as Libya, as well as other states including Pakistan, Iran and Syria,[29] thereby giving rise to US fears and providing justification (in Washington's eyes) for regional missile defences.

Strategically, China sees even a limited American NMD system deployed in Alaska as an attempt to diminish its own small strategic missile force, and with it any deterrent value in its relations with the United States or in a future conflict. In its opposition, China has called the proposed NMD "a threat to international security and stability" and "a tool of superpower hegemony" by the world's sole superpower — a position which is supported by Russia. And like Russia, China has criticized the United States for seeking revisions to the 1972 ABM in order to deploy its proposed NMD system. But China, in turn, has been criticized for its stance. For example, the Japanese Defence Agency's National Institute for Defence Studies, in its just-released annual *East Asian Strategic Review*, noted that "it is not acceptable that...[China] criticizes a country [like Japan] which possesses no ballistic missiles for conducting research on Theater Missile Defence."[30] In addition, there are suggestions that China is striving to create an anti-missile system of its own with the deployment of Russian-built SA-300 missiles around Beijing and the port of Tientsin. But diplomatic reports from Beijing suggest that none of the essential radar and computer components needed for such a system have been seen on the Chinese mainland.[31]

Prospects

In a recent article, Paul Bracken has argued that a TMD system to protect American forces deployed forward in the East Asia region would be useless as a defence system because it could be overwhelmed by cheaper offensive missiles. In addition, such a theater missile "Maginot Line" could provoke even larger offensive missile deployments in the region.[32]

While most American arguments for an NMD system centre on countering the developing North Korean missile threat, in fact China, with its small but operational ICBM delivery systems topped with miniaturized nuclear warheads and enhanced radiation weapons, could be cited just as well, a point noted by the state-run China Daily in Beijing.[33] Furthermore, China is understood to be developing a multi-warhead capacity for its missile systems. Globally, even a small missile force with multi-warhead capacity could almost certainly overwhelm a limited missile defence. Regionally, with its rapidly-growing numbers of medium-range, WMD-capable missiles, it seems certain that Chinese strategic forces could launch enough missiles on their designated target to ensure an unacceptable level of damage — whether it would be Taiwan's command-and-control infrastructure or a US carrier battle group in the East Asian region.

In addition to strategic political questions like whether deploying an

NMD or a TMD system would only lead to unstable and expensive arms races, there are a number of technological questions. These include whether interceptor missiles can be developed to accurately "hit-to-kill" incoming missiles, particularly in view of the lack of successful tests to date; whether there will be an unacceptable level of technology failures and software problems; whether cheap countermeasures and decoys will "defeat" any missile defences, and whether the rising cost estimates will halt even a limited missile defence.

There are also the various country factors. In recent months, there have been a number of significant changes within the East Asian region. A new opposition Democratic Progressive Party government will take over power in Taiwan from the KMT party which has ruled the island for 50 years. In Japan, a new prime minister has taken office due to the recent death of his predecessor: South Korea's legislative elections failed to produce a majority for President Kim Dae-jung and may adversely affect his "Sunshine Policy" with North Korea, especially at the forthcoming historic June 2000 leadership summit in Pyongyang.

[Editor's note: the Pyongyang summit saw the two Koreas agree to open talks on a range of bilateral issues, holding out the possibility for reduced tensions. North Korean leader Kim Jong Il announced that he would undertake a trip to the South "when the time was right."]

What does appear certain is that, when the leaders of the seven major industrialized democracies plus Russia meet in Japan's southern island of Okinawa for the July 2000 G7+1 Summit, the American NMD program and the American-supported TMD for East Asia will be a contentious topics. Russian president Vladimir Putin has already stated that Russia is opposed to amending the ABM treaty to permit the deployment of missile interceptors in Alaska. Given the congruence of Moscow's national security interests with those of China — particularly its opposition to "sole superpower hegemony" — and its increasing sales of sophisticated armaments to Beijing, Russia and China appear to be united in their opposition to NMD. Such a system — as well as a TMD system in East Asia — would deny China much of the diplomatic and military leverage that it has sought from its costly development of a strategic missile force, in both its bilateral relations with the United States and as a deterrent to a unilateral declaration of independence by Taiwan. At present, a limited NMD system is more relevant to countering China's current missile force than North Korea's projected missile development in the next few years.

As a writer wrote recently with regards to Europe and missile defences, "money and technology cannot remake geography."[34] The same can be said for East Asia, as Japan, South Korea and Taiwan are geographically close — with reaction time counted in a couple of minutes — to medium- or long-range missile launches from North Korea or even China. To ensure security and stability in East Asia in the face of missile-antimissile escalation, it may become necessary to work toward a missile reduction scheme such as took place in Europe in the 1980s in response to the Soviet deployment of its SS-20 medium-range missiles in communist Eastern Europe. Negotiations ultimately resulted in the 1987 Intermediate Nuclear Forces (INF) Accord which eliminated an entire category of nuclear weapons from the front-line between NATO and the Warsaw Pact and brought about a reduction in regional tensions.

Notes

1. George J. Tenet, Director of Central Intelligence, "The Worldwide Threat in 2000: Global Realities of US National Security" and Vice-Admiral Thomas R. Wilson, Director of Defense Intelligence Agency, "Military Threats and Security Challenges though 2015," testimony before the US Senate Select Committee on Intelligence, Washington DC, 2 February 2000.

2. Damien McElroy, "US boosts defences of North Korea's nervous neighbours," *Daily Telegraph* (London), 1 August 1999.

3. For background, see Robert D'A. Henderson, "SDI and the NATO Allies," in *Perspectives on the Arms Race*, ed. David Carlton and Carlo Schaerf (London: Macmillan Publishers, 1989), 169-90.

4. For example, see David Fairhall, "Eschewing the Scud," *The Guardian* (London), 12 March 1997 and Robert Wall, "Future of Missile Defences lies in Advanced Technology," *Aviation Week & Space Technology* (New York), 16 August 1999, 71-73.

5. Nigel Holloway, "Asian Star Wars: Debate heats up over East Asian missile defence," *Far Eastern Economic Review* (Hong Kong), 6 June 1996, 20-21 and Robert D'A. Henderson, "Continuing Tensions in the Taiwan Straits," *CISS Strategic Datalink,* No. 85, January 2000.

6. According to two Japanese parliamentarians, North Korea apparently used a high proportion of Japanese technology and equipment in its Taepo Dong missiles — with much of it bought off-the-shelf in Tokyo's electronics mecca, the Akihabara district. They highlighted this point in their demand for tightened Japanese foreign exchange regulations and trade legislation." See Andrew Cornell, "Japanese politicians call for greater national security," *Australian Financial Review* (Sidney), 29 July 1999.

7. "Japan urged to consider regional stability in spy-satellite project," *Korea Herald* (Seoul), 11 January 1999.

8. Don Kirk, "US and Japan to join in missile defence to meet Pyongyang threat," *International Herald Tribune* (Paris), 29 July 1999.

9. "Cabinet OK's antimissile study with US," *Japan Times* (Tokyo), 13 August 1999; Juliet Hindell, "US shield to cover Japan," *Daily Telegraph* (London), 14 August 1999; and Munehiro Hirata, "Cabinet's TMD policy unclear," *Mainichi Daily News* (Tokyo), 21 November 1999.

10. This was cited as one of the prime reasons Israel developed its OFEK satellite series — with its OFEK 3 regional reconnaissance satellite being

launched in April 1995; *New York Times*, 6 April 1995.

11. *Asahi Shimbun* (Tokyo), 23 May 1996 and Kyodo News Service news report, Tokyo, 23 May 1996. Also see Robert D'A. Henderson, "Reforming Japanese Intelligence," *International Journal of Intelligence and CounterIntelligence* 10, no. 2 (summer 1997): 227-38.

12. "IKONOS reduces need for spy satellite project," *Yomiuri Shimbun* (Tokyo), 4 November 1999. Launched in September 1999, IKONOS is the world's highest-resolution imaging satellite for commercial use. The Lockheed Martin Corporation, along with other companies including Japan's Mitsubishi Corporation, founded Space Imaging Inc. in 1998. There are already plans for a next-generation IKONOS 2 satellite with a proposed 50 centimetre resolution to be launched in 2003.

13. Jun Kwan-woo, "Seoul reaffirms no plan to join US-led theater missile defense plan," *Korea Herald*, 4 May 1999.

14. Jun Kwan-woo, "Seoul's missile development gains momentum," *Korea Herald*, 13 July 1999 and "US boosts defences of North Korea's nervous neighbours," *Daily Telegraph*, 1 August 1999.

15. Jun Kwan-woo, "Instead of TMD, Seoul needs other [short-range] system," *Korea Herald*, 19 April 1999 and "Pentagon proposes US$4.2 billion arms deal with ROK," *The Korea Times* (Seoul), 10 November 1999. In addition, a number of the existing PAC-2 batteries in South Korea — and in the Middle East as well — were found to have technical faults and had to be replaced; "Defective US air defense missiles replaced," Associated Press news report, Washington DC, 23 March 2000.

16. For example, see the signed commentary in the Korean Workers Party newspaper Nodong Sinmun — on the North Korean news agency KCNA website, 6 February 2000.

17. "North Korea promises arms build-up to cope with TMD missile defense system," Agence France Presse news report, Paris, 1 September 1999.

18. "Top CIA analyst warns on Korean missiles," Associated Press news report, Washington DC, 10 February 2000 and "US and Japan vow to continue missile defence study," Agence France Presse news report, Tokyo, 16 February 2000.

19. "Taipei plans to build its own missile shield," Agence France Press news report, Taipei, 23 August 1999.

20. See Henderson, "Continuing Tensions in the Taiwan Straits."

21. For example, "US arms control pull-back threatens world peace," *China Daily* (Beijing), 14 January 2000.

22. "DPP presidential candidate favours Taiwan joining TMD," Central News Agency news report, Taipei, 3 November 1999 and Wu Tian-jung, "DPP urges support for TMD technology transfer," *Chung-Kuo Shih-Pao* (Taipei), 6 December 1999.

23. Alice Hung, "Taiwan's Chen hopeful of buying US destroyers," Reuters news report, Taipei, 19 April 2000.

24. Nikkei news report, Washington D.C., 29 April 2000

25. "Taiwan wants to develop long-range missiles," Agence France Presse news report, Taipei, 8 December 1999 and "Tang: Long-range missiles not policy," United Daily News report, Taipei, 10 December 1999. Tang Fei has been nominated as the prime minister in president-elect Chen Shui-bian's bipartisan cabinet.

26. *China Daily* (Beijing), 26 November 1999.

27. See Robert D'A. Henderson, "Will China use force against Taiwan?" *CISS Strategic Datalink*, No. 86, February 2000 and Robert Kagan, "How China will take Taiwan," Washington Post, 12 March 2000.

28. "China's Vice-Premier warns Taiwanese independence will mean war," Xinhua News Agency news report, Beijing, 28 January 2000.

29. Sue Lackey, "Syria gains forbidden missile technology from China," ABCNEWS news report, Washington D.C., 23 August 1999 and Bill Gertz, "China 'is helping Libya on missiles'," *Washington Times*, 13 April 2000.

30. "Japanese think-tank slams Chinese 'hegemony'," *Hong Kong Standard*, 10 March 2000.

31. "China said to be building anti-missile system," Reuters news report, Beijing, 19 November 1999.

32. Paul Bracken, "America's Maginot Line," *The Atlantic Monthly* (Boston), December 1998, 85-93.

33. "US missile system designed to contain China, Chinese expert says," Agence France Presse news report, Beijing, 12 April 2000. In August 1999, China successfully tested its Dongfeng-31 ICBM with a range of 8,000 kms — capable of striking Alaska and Hawaii. It is currently developing a longer-range Dongfeng-41, which is expected to have a 12,000 kms

range — enough to hit most of continental United States and Europe; "China able to hinder US intervention in Strait Crisis," *Sing Tao Jih Pao* (Hong Kong), 5 October 1999 and "New ballistic missile tested in China," Associated Press news report, Hong Kong, 16 October 1999.

34. Philip Stephens, "An Umbrella against the World," *Financial Times* (London), 13 April 2000.

THE EUROPEAN DIMENSION OF BALLISTIC MISSILE DEFENCE

Dr. Jim Fergusson

There is one significant aspect of the missile defence debate that has largely been ignored, downplayed, misread or misunderstood in Canada. This relates to the limited press coverage of the European position on ballistic missile defence (BMD) in general and National Missile Defence (NMD) in particular. For many in Canada, such as Foreign Minister Lloyd Axworthy, European opposition to NMD is being used to buttress opposition to Canadian participation in NMD. However, the attempt to draw upon European opposition in Canada ignores two key points. First, the rhetoric from Europe reported in the press implies a consensus among the Europeans in opposition to NMD. The second concerns the relationship between this rhetoric and the reality of missile defence developments in Europe itself. This reality has been hidden or masked, at least in the media, and has certainly been downplayed by the Europeans, and to a lesser degree by NATO as well. The reality of missile defence tells an entirely different story of what's going on in Europe. Accordingly, I will conclude this presentation by suggesting, very bluntly, that the way Canada has understood Europe, or the way that Europe has been interpreted on BMD, is not only counter-productive to Canadian strategic interests, but in fact misses the whole point.

Let me begin with the rhetoric and relate it to reality. First (and this will not be surprising to any of the NATO-watchers here) there is really no single voice or agreed viewpoint on European concerns about NMD. As expected, there is significant variance in the concerns expressed by the NATO allies. The reality is that the Europeans are investing, albeit at comparatively low levels when compared to the United States, in missile defence systems, primarily in conjunction with their new generation of

---

Dr. Jim Fergusson is Professor of political science at the University of Manitoba.

naval air defence vessels, particularly frigates. However, expectations are that the United Kingdom, for example, will develop and deploy its new Type-45 destroyer with an initial lower tier, endoatmospheric missile defence capability, that could subsequently be up-graded to an upper-tier, exoatmospheric, or theatre missile defence (TMD), capability. In turn, the Type-45 destroyer will have the ability to integrate into the American naval-based lower and upper tier systems, which are expected to be online sometime between the middle and end of this decade. Finally, alongside the United Kingdom programme, as well as other European programs briefly discussed later, there are also developments occurring within NATO. These are centred upon the modernisation of NATO's air command and control system (ACCS), and the concept of Extended Air Defence (EAD).

The modernisation of NATO's ACCS is now moving forward, with the first phase set to be completed sometime in the middle of the decade. With it comes the start of two initial feasibility studies regarding the proposed development of a NATO EAD capability. EAD will be directly linked through ACCS and the US early warning and missile defence command and control systems to create what NATO calls an Extended Integrated Air Defence (EIAD) capability for the alliance. Importantly, EAD and EIAD, as the replacement for the old NATO Integrated Air Defence System (NATINADS), is simply acquiring a lower and upper tier missile defence capability integrated into the traditional air defence one. It is an interesting term, because it is the NATO code for missile defence, and in a way part of the "masking" of missile defence in the public discourse.

On the basis of this reality, it is useful to talk a bit about European opposition, or concerns about NMD. Similar in many ways to Canada, the Europeans appeared to wake up to the NMD issue, at least publicly, in the fall of 1999. At that time, the first formal briefings to the North Atlantic Council (NAC) were given by a range of US officials, including Secretary of Defense Cohen, and Under-Secretaries of State Holum and Talbot. As part of these briefings, US officials agreed to keep the allies briefed on NMD developments and arms control negotiations with Russia on amending the ABM Treaty, and START III in Geneva. Since then, there has been repeated public criticism of NMD, primarily led by the French. Despite the general criticism, there is no consensus view among Europeans of the problems concerning NMD. Rather, there are a range of different views and concerns which combine into the public appearance of consensus. More importantly, I would argue that the Europeans have also attempted to mask their real interests with regard to missile defence under the umbrella of their so-called opposition.

Not surprisingly, when you look at the public opposition, France is the most critical, whereas Turkey is, in fact, most supportive. Nonetheless, my remarks will primarily focus on the 'big four': the United Kingdom, Italy, France and Germany. At one level, all raise the same set of concerns, but the way they see and weigh them varies significantly. The concerns consist of the ballistic missile threat, the nature of proliferation, the viability of deterrence, strategic de-coupling and differential security, Russia, arms control and non-proliferation, and the issue of alliance management. But the 'big four' do not perceive all of them as necessarily problematic relative to NMD. First of all, with regards to the matter of the ballistic missile threat, the French are the most vocal, and essentially argue that there is no threat. Testing a long range missile, as North Korea has done, does not mean an operational capability. Moreover, they perceive little likelihood that North Korea, or the Iran, Iraq, and Libya, will develop an actual operational capability to threaten Europe, or, for that matter, North America, in any meaningful way until well into the next decade.

The British, on the other hand, tend to agree with the American threat assessment. They are deeply concerned about the improving technical ballistic missile capabilities of these states, and are concerned about the transfer of technology from North Korea to countries such as Libya and others. However, the British break company with the Americans by arguing that capabilities must be related to political intent. Even though missile technology is proliferating, it is not necessarily the case that these so-called "rogue states" will actually move to threaten directly either Europe or North America. Thus given a threat assessment, which approximates elements of both the French and American view, the United Kingdom prefers to slow down the time line concerning NMD deployment.

Yet, despite the French and British perspectives on the missile threat, there is consensus in NATO on the threat posed by proliferation. In 1994, the Senior Political and Senior Defence Groups on Proliferation were created at the Brussels Summit in 1994. Most recently, this has been demonstrated in the emphasis placed on proliferation at last year's NATO summit in Washington, and with the creation early this year of a NATO Centre on proliferation. In effect, then, the issue of the threat is not *if* it will appear, but rather *when*. It is a debate on timing.

Part of the threat debate is assessments of the motives of states to acquire ballistic missiles, potentially married to weapons of mass destruction. European critics of NMD have argued that these states are largely motivated by regional concerns. The classic example is Iran, which recently conducted its second test of the Shahab-3 medium range ballistic missile, being motivated by the legacy of Iraqi Scud attacks during the Iran-Iraq war. There are also concerns among the Persian Gulf Arab states who regard all ballistic missile programs, including those of Israel, Egypt, and Libya, with concern. Hence, some critics in Europe suggest that NMD deployment may actually spur the development of longer range missiles. However, it is difficult to see how this motive operates, especially when considering that one of the security challenges faced by these states is the fear of US led intervention.

For the French, and to a lesser degree the British, the missile proliferation issue raises the question about the viability of deterrence. The French and the British, as well as others, believe that they can ultimately rely on nuclear deterrence for their security. However, this is a concern for the Italians, who had Libyan missiles launched against the island of Lampeusa in 1986. The French believe that their nuclear forces can deter the use of *all* weapons of mass destruction — nuclear, biological, and chemical. In contrast, the British limit their deterrent's utility to nuclear threats. They posit that a nuclear deterrent threat is not proportionate for chemical and biological weapons. In contrast to both, the US have deep concerns about the utility of nuclear deterrence, and also suggests that deployed missile defences actually reinforce deterrence, rather than undermine it. At minimum, missile defence provides another option, rather than strictly relying upon nuclear retaliation.

These three issues spill into the question of strategic de-coupling, and what the Europeans now call differential security. Interestingly, this is a point that has been emphasized most by the Italians. Since they are not under the formal umbrella of either the French or British nuclear forces, the Italians are deeply concerned (because of their geo-political location) that NMD will result in the de-coupling of US strategic forces from European security. This old argument, which dates back to the ABM and SDI debates, thus creates 'different levels of security" between Europe and the US, and within Europe itself. A US defended by NMD will have a higher level of security than the Europeans, that could undermine alliance solidarity, consensus and co-operation. The British, however, recognize that "differential security" has always existed among the members of the alliance. Today, Turkey in particular has perhaps the lowest level of security relative to the ballistic missile threat from the south, and security levels grow as one moves north and west. The United Kingdom, Turkey, and to a lesser degree Germany, do not really buy into the differential security case, in contrast to Italy and France.

There is, of course, the issue of Russia. The impact of NMD on the west's relationship with Russia is the fundamental concern of Germany. Despite the damage done to this relationship as a result of NATO enlargement, and western policy towards the Balkans in general, and Kosovo in particular, Germany is deeply concerned that NMD will have a dramatic impact on the potential for improved cooperative relations with Moscow. Hence, any movement towards NMD deployment must be done within a cooperative, negotiated framework with Russia. To a lesser degree, the French echo this sentiment. The United Kingdom, however, seems least concerned about the Russian dimension. NMD does not in any way undermine the viability of Russian strategic forces and their deterrent capability. Thus, Russia opposition is largely politically driven — a bargaining chip — rather than strategically substantive.

Russia naturally spills into perspectives on the ABM Treaty issue, and arms control/non-proliferation in general. The most interesting view about the ABM treaty comes from the French. They are the most firm supporters of maintaining the treaty as it exists. They voted in favour of strict Treaty maintenance and adherence in the Russian-Chinese sponsored resolution before the United Nations First Committee and General Assembly; the only ally to do so, with the rest abstaining. In addition, one of the concerns is not the ABM treaty itself, but the potential implications of a negotiated amended Treaty, that could entail cooperative technology exchange and American support to the Russian missile defence program; in other words, the longstanding fear of a Russo-American deal struck over Europe's head with significant implications for France's nuclear forces.

This French fear is in many ways a legacy from the Cold War. There are other views about the ABM treaty, but generally the rest of the Europeans agree that any Russo-American deal on ABM is fine. In this sense, the European view on the ABM Treaty issue is identical to the Canadian foreign affairs one. The Treaty is vital and must continue, but its specifics are left to the US and Russia.

There are also some issues raised about the impact of missile defence on the whole non-proliferation regime and the Comprehensive Test Ban

Treaty (CTBT) in light of the US Senate's rejection. In addition, there are also concerns about the future direction of the US NMD programme. These, of course, query whether NMD is the first step towards implementing Reagan's SDI. They are, however, fairly minor issues, but part of the litany of concerns that the Europeans have, and will likely continue to raise.

The final issue, which they all agree on to a greater or lesser degree, is the issue of alliance management. The concern among many of the Europeans, primarily led by the United Kingdom, is that NMD could significantly damage cooperation among the allies. It could serve to undermine the transatlantic relationship, give a boost to those in Europe who support the European Security and Defence Identity (ESDI) as distinct from ESDI as the European pillar of NATO, and push Europe towards politically de-coupling from the US and North America. This is certainly the major concern of the United Kingdom, with strong support from the Germans.

In brief, these are the range of concerns expressed by Canada's European allies. Certainly, the European perspectives on NMD are much more detailed, nuanced, and complicated than I can present today. Nonetheless, significant differences exist among the Europeans within the general consensus of concerns about NMD.

With these range of concerns in mind, let us now turn to the reality of the European missile defence programs. The European programs are primarily, but not exclusively, naval-based, and lower-tier systems. As noted in the introduction, the UK Type-45 air-defence destroyer under development will deploy a lower-tier system, by employing the trinational (British-Franco-Italian) Principal Anti-Air Missile (PAAMS): the Aster 30. Furthermore, given British naval requirements, one can expect the British to upgrade eventually to an upper tier, theatre missile defence capability, using either the next generation of Aster, or the US Standard Missile (SM) III when they become available. Such an upgrade would provide a theatre-wide defence capability not only for deployed forces, but also for the protection of the United Kingdom itself from intermediate range missiles. Of particular interest is the United Kingdom's Sampson tracking and guidance radar for the Type-45, that is based upon the MESAR system. This system is about to begin its next series of tests in co-operation with the US at White Sands, New Mexico. This close co-operation, alongside the US naval programs, is a good indicator of the eventual acquisition of a theatre capability.

The Franco-Italian Horizon frigate program (to which the UK was a partner until it opted for the purely national Type-45) will also provide a lower-tier missile defence capability. Part of the problem in the original Horizon programme was different naval requirements, and different beliefs with regards to what missile defence was required for these frigates. The French and the Italians had a different view from the British. They all agreed there was need for a missile defence capability, but the program fell apart due to disagreement over exactly the type of capability relative to the design of the platform. As noted earlier, the three allies will deploy the PAAMS Aster 30, and possibly its follow-on, the Aster 45 which is projection as an upper tier, or exoatmospheric kinetic-kill interceptor (the Aster-30 employs a conventional proximity blast kill). The French and the Italians have also raised the possibility of the Aster-30 as a viable European alternative to the current American proposal to use the Patriot interceptor for the ground-based NATO Medium Extended Air Defence (MEAD) program.

However, it's not just the French, the Italians and the British that are involved in missile defence. There is also the loose tri-national Dutch-German-Spanish frigate program; all with a similar hull design, but employing different types of components. Importantly, all plan to employ the US SM-II, which can readily be upgraded to the SM-II, Block IVA lower tier interceptor missile, as well as further down the road to the SM-III upper tier interceptor. The Dutch and the Germans are developing APAR radar guidance system, whereas Spain is planning to acquire the US Spy-I radar, currently used by the Aegis Class Cruisers and Destroyers. Of note, Canada is involved in the APAR research project as well, purportedly for a potential upgrade to its frigates' radar, or possibly for the replacement of the Tribal Class Air Defence destroyer in the future.

Turning to ground-based missile defence, the NATO-MEAD program has been troubled ever since the French pulled out in 1997. Consisting of Germany, Italy, and the US, MEAD is being designed to provide a mobile 360-degree lower-tier intercept capability for deployed forces in the field, possibly using the Patriot interceptor. Concerns about the US commitment to the program, which has entered the design stage, still exist, so that the future of MEAD remains open. Besides MEAD, it should also be noted that both Germany and the Netherlands currently deploy the Patriot Advanced Capability-2 (PAC-2), and have expressed interest in acquiring PAC-3, which will be entering into service shortly. For Germany, deploying PAC-3 as a replacement for PAC-2 and as the interceptor for MEADS hinges on the technology transfer issues, with Washington hesitating to pass on technical information considered vital by Berlin. This is not a problem for the Dutch at all. Finally, Greece has expressed interest in PAC-3, and Turkey has also expressed interest in both PAC-3 and the Israeli Arrow theatre system. Acquisition of the Arrow depends upon US agreement, as it paid a significant portion of the Arrow's development costs, and has a veto on any sales of the system.

So there, very briefly, are the European missile defence programs. The focus on low-tier systems are partially driven by the lack of mature technologies, a desire to see how the American programs evolve, and significant budget constraints relative to other pressing military modernisation requirements. Regardless, the European programs are being designed to ensure their interoperability with American systems coming on stream over this decade. In addition, they will also possess the capacity to be upgraded to a theatre missile defence capability. Such a capability relative to emerging missile threats to Europe from the Middle East and south Mediterranean littoral will provide Europe in the future with a limited strategic defence capability. Moreover, the requirement for a strategic defence has already been recognized, notwithstanding the anti-NMD rhetoric.

The 1999 NATO Strategic Concept from the Washington Summit makes two points about missile defence. First, within the context of Article V (collective defence), it points out the emerging proliferation (ballistic missile) threat to the populations and territories of Europe. Second, there is direct reference to the need for flexible, mobile, sustainable missile defence capabilities for non-Article V operations. In addition, missile defence is one of the elements of the Defence Capabilities Initiative (DCI); a program which calls on NATO members to co-ordinate investment in capabilities that are expected to be key for future military requirements.

Alongside this policy foundation, there are a variety of major developments within NATO itself. As I mentioned earlier, the modernisation of the ACCS is underway, and as part of this programme, the alliance's peripheral radars in the south will acquire an upper-tier tracking capability. ACCS is designed to be interoperable with US systems, and NATO has also implemented the first phase of the US offer to provide early warning data, which is vital for missile defence. In addition planners at NATO headquarters and Supreme Headquarters Allied Powers Europe (SHAPE) are emphasising the importance of weaning European naval capabilities away from the defence of individual ships (which by and large has been the preoccupation of the Europeans) into a theatre defence framework. This theatre framework will ensure naval capabilities are linked directly into ACCS to provide direct support to a co-ordinated European defence for Article V and non-Article V operations.

Finally, there is the aforementioned EAD initiative. Last February, the NAC approved a Stand Alone Project under the auspices of the NATO Command, Control, and Consultation Agency in the Hague to conduct feasibility studies on EAD for the development of an initial capability by 2010. There are four pillars to EAD: conventional counter-force/ potential pre-emption; a lower-tier capability; an upper-tier capability, and air-based boost phase intercept. Two feasibility studies will be undertaken by separate industrial consortia, that should be completed in 2003.

With the nature of the European programs, and the evolving command and control/battle management role of NATO in missile defence, it is important to try to understand European concerns about NMD. This may appear counter-intuitive given the legacy of the way we have come to think about Europe, but European concerns are not so much a legacy of the great public debates of the eighties against Euromissiles and SDI. Rather, the European rhetoric is largely driven by a fear that if the US moves too quickly and deploys NMD, that it would ignite within Europe increasing public demands for a serious investment in missile defence. Such demands would function from the reality that Europe will be threatened by so-called "rogue states" (in fact, parts of Europe already are) before North America. If NMD is deployed, the reality becomes North America with a defence but little threat, and Europe without a defence, but with a threat.

There are also concerns about generating a public debate in a period where little public attention is being paid to defence and security threats. The emphasis on the threat (Alliance solidarity), and the "rogue states" argument, could catch fire, prompt demands for investments in strategic defences for Europe, and raise wider concerns relative to asymmetric threats (terrorism, etc.). Given demands on the defence budgets of the governments and the other European political interests, their opposition to NMD really serves to keep missile defence on the back burner for the time being. Nonetheless, the evidence clearly shows that Europe is moving down the missile defence path. The desire among the Europeans is to slow the US NMD program down, rather than actually stop the development and deployment of a limited NMD for North America. Even for those truly opposed to NMD, they are likely to recognize that NMD can not be stopped given the domestic political dynamic in the US.

The rhetoric and reality of Europe thus has implications for Canadian policy deliberations. I would like to make three very brief points. First, Canada, as the Europeans, are much too late to influence the US decision-making process on NMD. In fact, if you go back to ABM and SDI, the allies very rarely take the initiative and attempt to influence the American political process. Moreover, the American political process is by and large driven by domestic political debates, and allied viewpoints are largely fodder for this debate. Thus, if either Europe or Canada think that they are going to move the US at this point in time, the answer is no. If you go back to the four criteria of the Clinton Administration for deployment — threat, cost, feasibility, allies and international security — there is only one left to be checked off that's of any meaning: feasibility. It will probably be decided as a function of the next intercept test in June. *[Editor's note: the July, 2000 flight test failed to intercept the target when the exoatmospheric interceptor, or "kill vehicle", failed to separate from its rocket booster. As the test was intended to assess the ability of the interceptor's sensor suite to distinguish between the target warhead and decoys, the fact that the test never proceeded to this stage leaves unanswered the question of whether the entire system is technologically mature].*

Second, NMD is not about US unilateralism, it is not about withdrawal, and it is not about Fortress America. It is *a* if not *the* key to the evolving US strategy of engagement, as enunciated repeatedly by the Clinton Administration. It is vital for the political coupling of the United States to Europe, especially relative to internal US politics. It is central when you look from the US outward to the future of the transatlantic relationship. NMD is therefore vital for Canada, or at least for the transatlantic pillar of Canadian foreign and defence policy. Moreover, in this context, it becomes very counterproductive for Canada to in fact attempt to engage the Europeans as a means to oppose NMD.

The final, and perhaps the most important point, is about theatre missile defence within the conceptual context of the ABM/Cold War definition of strategic weapons. Partially as a function of the September 1997 demarcation agreements between Russia and the US, theatre missile defences have been separated from strategic ones, and have been politically legitimized. On the technical basis of demarcation, theatre is not strategic. But, theatre missile defence capabilities will serve a strategic role for Europe. Thus hidden by the NMD debate, one is really talking about a slow, evolutionary development/deployment process in which Europe *will* develop and deploy a strategic defence for all of Europe sometime in the future. For Canada, therefore, this future reality raises significant implications of the political fallout of a negative decision by Canada on NMD participation. Canada could pay a political price, which the Europeans won't. They have their own interests and motives for opposing NMD for now, while they continue down the path of missile defence at a much slower rate, with smaller investments in key technologies, and with less public fanfare.

FACTORS AFFECTING CANADA'S APPROACH TO NATIONAL MISSILE DEFENCE

The Honourable Art Eggleton

Let me begin by thanking David Rudd and the Canadian Institute of Strategic Studies for inviting me here to share my views on National Missile Defence. I'm happy to be a part of this seminar because I think we can all agree that well-informed discussion from all points of view is healthy. Seminars like this help to put the issues out for public view, and that's important at this point in time as we are getting closer and closer to the United States' decision on this matter, and of course that affects Canada and a decision on our part in the matter.

Before I get to National Missile Defence *per se*, let me put it in a bit of a broader context — specifically that of 'homeland defence'. Homeland defence is a phrase I have heard quite frequently coming up from the United States; it encompasses a number of things, not all of them directly relevant to military or defence matters. Homeland defence deals with criminality, illegal entry into the United States, the concern of terrorist activities, cyber attacks, and a wide range of other areas that the United States is becoming more cognizant of as potential threats. The United States has, in the last hundred years, fought in two world wars and numerous other conflicts, but none of those were on its soil (with the exception, of course, of the Pearl Harbour attack). None directly affected the continental United States. But there is a growing concern that some of the things that are happening in the world in terms of defence and security issues could affect them directly now.

For example, an issue that has preoccupied the US for a number of years has been illegal drugs coming into the United States from various parts of the world. They're concerned not only with drugs entering the

---

The Honourable Art Eggleton is Minister of National Defence.

country from their seas on either side, but from their neighbours to the north and south. I think we can all agree that we don't want them in our country either, we don't want them going from our country to the United States, and we would want to work closely with the Americans on that kind of security issue.

With respect to terrorism, last December, when two people of Algerian nationality went from Canada into the United States, concerns were expressed about the possibility of terrorists coming over the border. A lot of the discussion that goes on in the United States is focused on their southern border. Still, there are concerns about the northern border, to the point where we've seen in recent years — in the Congress in particular — policy proposals that might tighten up the border. Any tightening of the border has to be of concern for us, because we have a great deal of commerce (more than a billion dollars a day) going between Canada and the United States. Some 43% of our economy is dependent on trading, and almost 90% of that trade is with the United States. So we have to be concerned about anything that might affect our common border.

Another area of concern that has recently been at the forefront has been what is called the International Trade in Arms Regulations (ITARs), which deals with defence products. We have a very integrated defence industry in Canada and the United States. Sometimes some of the defence products go back and forth between a parent company and a subsidiary or between two affiliates. We have had no difficulty with this for a number of years because we have had a very special relationship with the United States in the area of defence production. Of course, this only reflects the very wide relationship we have with them in many other areas of defence. Recently the discussions about tightening up in the ITARs have been of considerable concern to us because it affects a $50-billion industry and a great many jobs in this country. It looks like we may be well on our way to working that out, but it has not been easy. The United States has been very concerned about how we deal with these secure military products that are going back and forth between our two countries.

Most recently, we've seen the possibility of attacks on computer systems. Today's arrest in Montreal points out how cyber-attacks easily travel across borders — with a great degree of integration comes a great degree of concern about the security of information systems. The US is also concerned about terrorists carrying out attacks such as were seen at the World Trade Centre in New York or in the Tokyo subway system. The possibility of chemical or biological weaponry being a threat on

American soil is another area of concern and therefore comes under the umbrella area of homeland defence.

Of course the development and proliferation of weapons of mass destruction, as well as the development and proliferation of delivery systems, also forms part of the concern about homeland defence. I think a point to be made here is that we do not want a 'Fortress America' kind of mentality to develop. This would result in a US perception that, within its own borders, it has to have maximum protection, even to the exclusion of its good friend and neighbour to the north. We would prefer to look at the entire perimeter of the continent as being within the scope of protection. We want to work together on the defence and security of North America as a whole, not just have the United States batten down the hatches, look inward and create this kind of fortress mentality. I think we would have considerable agreement on both sides of the border about dealing with most of these issues together, in a cooperative way, through the perimeter protection of our continent.

Ballistic Missile Defence is another area of concern for the United States. As I'm sure you've heard this morning, a decision could be made very shortly on this matter. If the June test proves to be successful from a technical standpoint, it could well lead to a decision by the President, even before the election. He may decide he wants to take it out of the hands of the candidates in the presidential election, take it out of the political forum and deal with it right away. There is going to be a lot of political consideration of the decision that he makes by the autumn. On the other hand, he could leave it to a new president, and there are those who suggest that should be done because it would be pushing it too fast otherwise. But a lot will depend on how the testing comes out in June.

The Americans believe that they have to proceed with this kind of protection — if they can perfect the technology. It is by no means perfect, it doesn't cover cruise missiles or people bringing suitcases of weapons of mass destruction into the US. It could have numerous other flaws as well, but they're looking at it as one of the pieces in the puzzle, one of the things that they believe will afford them a greater defence against ballistic missiles. The US looks at the development of weapons systems in North Korea and sees that the capability for the North to reach farther and farther afield is being developed. They're concerned not only about North Korea, but about the sale of some of this missile technology and its weaponry to "rogue" regimes in other parts of the world. They're concerned about Iraq, or Iran, or Libya being able to buy or obtain some of this technology.

The US looks upon the fact that there is a capability as being a threat. In Canada, we tend to look at capability as just one aspect of the matter. We say, well, they're capable but is there a probability, is there a likelihood that this may actually happen? But the Americans tend to say, well, if there is a capability then there is a threat and we need to do something about it. And they expect that this capability could well develop in the years ahead.

This then brings us to the question of what we should do. If the continental United States is threatened, then Canada is threatened, because we are adjacent to the continental United States. The US has not formally asked us to participate at this point in time, and of course they haven't made a decision themselves, so it would be premature for us to make a decision now. But they're looking for our support; I think they've made that quite obvious. There's also the question of how this relates to NORAD. We have that agreement which is just now up for renewal. NORAD is already, of course, in a position to track any missile, any object, any plane that is coming toward the North American continent, and can track it in other places in the world too. So the capability already exists in terms of tracking this kind of weaponry, and presumably if a missile attack was launched against North America then NORAD would play a role in the warning phases because that's part of its current function. This then begs the question: does NORAD have a responsibility with respect to the interceptor missiles?

I think it's also important to understand, in terms of these interceptor missiles, as I'm sure you've heard before, that the Americans are talking about a very limited number of them. These are anti-missile missiles, interceptor missiles intended to be able to protect the United States against a *limited* ballistic missile attack — ballistic missiles carrying nuclear or chemical or biological warheads. NMD does not act as a deterrent with respect to the massive number of missiles that Russia continues to hold. As was the case throughout the Cold War, mutual deterrence is the way of dealing, in that particular case, with defence. In other words, the basis of defence is that both sides have more than enough to destroy each other and the world – mutual deterrence. So NMD does not affect that at all; it is a very limited number of interceptor missiles that would be used only in the case of an accidental launch or a rogue regime launch.

NMD is, I think, being incorrectly categorized as a revival of "Star Wars" — a Strategic Defence Initiative concept that goes back to the Reagan era. Well, that it is not. It is not Star Wars, nor is it Star Wars II.

It is land-based, with limited number of missiles. It would be used in case of a rogue regime or accidental or terrorist attack. It does not involve weaponry in space. Space obviously would be used as part of observation (it is now and will be in future) but not as a place to put the delivery systems.

So these are the issues that we have to look at in the context of how NMD affects arms control, disarmament, and our support for non-proliferation efforts. My colleague, Lloyd Axworthy [Minister of Foreign Affairs], has been talking about this of late, and of course the prime focus is with respect to the Anti-Ballistic Missile (ABM) treaty of 1972. That treaty would require amendment for NMD to be fielded — if the treaty is to be maintained — and the United States is in discussion with Russia about that very thing. I think there's a lot of hope about non-proliferation and arms control — the Russian Duma did recently ratify the START II agreement. But, at the same time, we wouldn't want to see, in the name of defence, something that creates international instability. So, the discussions that are going on regarding the ABM treaty and other aspects of arms control become very important. International instability as a product of putting in a defence system, such as National Missile Defence, is not a good trade-off. I think those are issues that have to be dealt with very seriously. By the same token, it is not a sure thing that such dire consequences would result if the United States deploys a National Missile Defence system. A limited number of defensive interceptors are not necessarily going to precipitate an arms race, or have the kind of consequences that perhaps some people have suggested. But I think we have to weigh all of these things very carefully. We have to look at both the defence aspect as well as the consequence to these international agreements on arms control.

For Canada, we also have to look at our relationship with the United States and our relationship with NORAD. Homeland defence, as I've described it, is an important area for us to be engaged in. That doesn't necessarily mean that we have to buy into National Missile Defence as part of homeland defence, but there are certainly a lot of other concerns in that homeland defence area that we should be working with the Americans quite closely on.

So these are the issues that we have to further concern ourselves with in this debate. As the Minister of National Defence, I certainly want to see the kind of discussion that is going on here continue throughout our country as we move down the road toward that point where we will be making a decision as to whether we are going to support the Americans in this matter. Supporting the Americans does not necessarily mean that we would have any missiles deployed on our soil. We have not been asked to do that. We have not been asked to contribute money either. We do, by the way, have a dialogue with the United States. We do have an involvement through our current policy – the 1994 White Paper raises the issue of missile defence – so we are already engaged in receiving information. But any decision to support the deployment is a decision that the government has yet to make and all of the issues that I've talked about here are a part of what we will have to consider in doing that.

Minister's Forum

Colonel Alain Pellerin, Conference of Defence Associations (CDA)

Inside the Cabinet, some have described your position as leaning forward on the issue of National Missile Defence (NMD), whereas your colleague, Minister Axworthy, is leaning backward. Would that be a fair description of the situation?

Minister Eggleton

He [Minister Axworthy] raises important issues, and the military and the Canadians we have in NORAD raise important issues. I think that we need to have a very careful examination of all of them. They are not mutually exclusive, dealing with defence issues on the one hand and dealing with international agreements on arms control and proliferation on the other. As I said, we wouldn't want to see international instability created as a result of any deployment, and I don't think the United States does either. So there are a lot of important issues to be dealt with and he [Minister Axworthy] raises a lot of them as well.

Peggy Mason, Canadian Council for International Peace and Security (CCIPS)

There's been a lot of discussion here on the limited nature of the intended deployment by the US if they decide to proceed with a National Missile Defence system. The *Washington Post* recently reported that, in light of Clinton's intention to travel to Moscow for a summit to try and work out an agreed amendment to the ABM treaty to allow such a limited deployment, 24 Senators, led by the Senate majority leader Trott, had indicated, in writing, their strongest opposition to any agreement between Russia and the United States that would limit the nature of the deployment of a National Missile Defence system. They said that the Senate would not agree to any such agreement. That, it seems to me, for Canada, leads to the worse possible situation — a decision to participate in the deployment of a system that will clearly be outside the Anti-Ballistic Missile (ABM) treaty. I wonder if you could comment on that. Given that it is this part of the US Senate that has driven this entire process, I don't think we can take their statements lightly.

Minister Eggleton

I think a lot of people are posturing right now. We have to see how the discussions go between the United States and Russia. Some will say that the ABM treaty is out of date, that it really is not a factor in the post-Cold War era. It may not be, strictly speaking, but on the other hand it is a symbol of the need to maintain the direction of arms reduction, arm control, non-proliferation. We've had a lot of proliferation in spite of all of these good efforts and good rhetoric, though. So I think we have to see how those discussions with Russia go. We, of course, will have to take that into consideration — how the ABM treaty ends up in this whole process — before we make a decision. That's one of the key pillars of our decision-making.

Laurence Baxter, CISS member

The question I have is regarding the possible ramifications of the NMD debate on the government's overall policy on foreign affairs and defence. There seems to be some indication of a disjuncture between DND and DFAIT on what constitutes foreign policy and defence. I realize that's a very big issues, especially considering human security, I wonder if you could comment on that any further (you did touch on it a bit already).

Minister Eggleton

Yes, in fact I thought that was the essence of what I was saying. We need to have a lot more discussion about this. That's why it's helpful to have seminars and debates like this. If you're asking me — and I think I was also being asked in the question a moment ago — how are you knocking each other back and forth in the Cabinet, no, I'm not going to tell you that.

Bill Watkins, Carleton University

Is DND planning on earmarking any defence dollars from the recent budget increase in expectation of a request from the United States to participate [in NMD]?

Minister Eggleton

Not specifically. We do have a joint-satellite project system that we are working on with the United States, and we are working on that system regardless of the decision on National Missile Defence. But if National Missile Defence is deployed, and if Canada becomes a part of it, then that system could lend itself to part of the surveillance system. But that is a separate matter and a separate decision has been taken on that.

David Zurawel

Minister, you highlighted how homeland defence sets the context for American defence policy. The Canada-US relationship — specifically the US International Trade in Arms Regulations (ITARs) — is something that we're concerned with. Is it within the government's power to allay US fears of illicit transfers of technology from Canadian companies, and so discourage the Americans from putting a stranglehold on cross-border defence trade.

Minister Eggleton

As I indicated in my remarks, quite aside from the issue of National Missile Defence, there are a number of other areas that are of concern, whether it's drugs or terrorists or any of their military secrets getting into the hands of other parties in other countries — rogue regimes or terrorists. So there are a number of areas that I don't think there would be any dispute that we can work with the Americans on. We need to take these concerns very seriously, and we need to work with them very carefully. Those are areas that if they feel that we are as concerned about those matters as they are – and we should be from our own security standpoint — then I think that mitigates against the kinds of measures that you're talking about. And I think we're well on our way, for example, in the ITARs, to being able to resolve [the matter] and continue to have this special status. But it's not something that we can take for granted and it's not something that should cause us to let down our efforts because there are a lot of people in the United States — whether it's in the administration or in the Congress — who watch these issues very closely, with great concern, since they affect their own security. I think we want to tell the United States that we want to work with them on a perimeter security of North America and not have them just feel that they have to pull back into a more fortress mentality. That is against our interests.

MORNING FORUM

Peggy Mason, Canadian Council for International Peace and Security (CCIPS)

Dr. Fergusson, since you didn't mention China in your presentation, I'd like you to comment as to whether or not the possible impact of a limited (or not) National Missile Defence deployment on China figures into European thinking at all. The other point I have to make is, I cannot let your remarks about the 'arbitrary distinction' between theatre missile defence and National Missile Defence go. Maybe it's arbitrary but it's enshrined in international treaties, and I would have thought that the difference between theatre and strategic was not exactly arbitrary. Of course, in narrow technical terms, you can make an argument that it's an arbitrary distinction but I think we're talking about a lot more than the narrow technical dimensions. If either or both of you want to comment on those issues...

Dr. Robert D'A. Henderson

The one point I'll quickly make in reply to you is that, though I did not cover Europe in my presentation, I have what I think is a rather interesting quote. This came from the *Financial Times*. A European writer recently wrote that "money and technology cannot remake geography." I mention it not so much for Europe but because I thought it was very appropriate for Asia. It reminded me very much of the SS-20 debate in the 1980s when the European allies in NATO did not seem to be as concerned as the United States was. Yes, the United States and the Soviet Union did reach an Intermediate Nuclear Forces (INF) Accord. This was excellent, as a whole category of missiles disappeared from the Cold War confrontation in Europe. In the Asian context the point is that Japan was only concerned when that North Korean missile went over top of it.

The session was chaired by David Rudd, CISS Executive Director.

There had been little interest in cabinet and almost less in the public domain. It all changed, and now they're on board, but it's worth noting that Japan was slow to join SDI — they took a long time to reach an agreement on economic and research benefits to come from the SDI research. They are doing the same with the theatre missile defences and so they are looking for technological benefits in addition to the national security.

Peggy Mason

Can I just add one element that wasn't said? That is, yes they're on board, but the Japanese have made it absolutely clear that they're on board for theatre missile defence *within* the confines of the ABM treaty and the government has reiterated that over and over and over again. I think that's important. They will not sign on if the treaty is abrogated, or if the Russians won't agree, or if the thing goes ahead outside the ABM treaty. The Japanese have consistently stated that TMD must be within the international treaty on this.

Dr. Henderson

I guess the catchphrase is theatre vs national. The ABM treaty covered the continental United States, I don't think it was ever hinted that it would cover US forces deployed abroad, bases, or US ships — particularly US carrier battle groups. Japan can say on the one hand, "We are fully in support of the ABM treaty" and yet on the other turn around and say, "We only have a theatre defence of our homeland, and we were never signatories to the ABM treaty."

Dr. Jim Fergusson

The first question about China — I'm not sure if you're asking about the impact of NMD on China or the Europeans' view of the China question. In most of the material I've looked at, and from the people I've talked to, when China emerges it emerges in the context of those who believe (and there are, of course, those in North America who believe it as well) that in fact NMD is designed against the Chinese. I myself don't agree with that argument, but outside of that sort of 'what the future is', the Europeans really are concerned primarily with the Russian issue and, as a function of geography, with threats from the Middle East.

Now, with regard to the arbitrary distinction between strategic and theatre, it's a Cold War distinction to start with, because the very way we thought about — and the way many still do think about — strategic, is in the context of the strategic relationship between the Soviet Union and the United States. The ABM treaty was constructed, of course, to constrain missile defences relative to long-range ballistic missiles and the only clear operational definition (at least from the ABM treaty) relates to testing in an ABM mode, and those are from the agreed statements, not within the actual text of the treaty itself. So it was a technical argument to start with.

Now, I think what Peggy is referring to is the demarcation agreement, signed by Russia and the United States but not ratified by Congress. The 24 Senators you talked about earlier are of that Republican group who believes the ABM treaty is defunct because Russia is not a successor to the Soviet Union. But that is another issue. The agreement enshrined the notion that the demarcation between theatre and strategic or National Missile Defence relates to the speed of the ballistic missiles. It relates to the speed of an ICBM traveling roughly 5000 kilometers and also to the speed of interceptors for lower-tier and upper-tier engagement. (There is no formal part of the agreement, only a statement on the part of the United States in 1997, about exactly how fast the upper-tier system would be). I agree with you entirely, the distinction is a political one and it's in the political interest of the Europeans and others to differentiate between a theatre defence and a strategic defence. But the fact of the matter, as I think my colleague pointed out in his maps, is that a naval-based system around Japan is a strategic defence for Japan, a naval based system around Taiwan is a strategic defence for Taiwan. As a study done in 1993 demonstrated, three naval taskforces based on Aegis class cruisers with lower and upper tier interceptors is a strategic defence for Europe against the Middle East. Finally, where this whole thing collapses, is if you have an Aegis-class upper-tier system task force (whether it is Japanese or an ally's) sitting in the sea of Japan, that system not only provides defence to Japan but also, depending upon the command and control, the communications systems, that system could potentially have a boost phase shot at a North Korean missile targeted for the United States. It could also potentially do a late-boost phase, if not likely a post-boost phase and mid-course phase shot for Chinese launch missiles. Everything starts to collapse in this area, I think we need to rethink that.

David Rudd

Are we saying then that if we distinguish between National Missile Defence, as something intended to protect the entire continental United

States, and theatre defence, as a sort of more portable local defence, we also have to bear in mind that theatre missile defence for a country the size of Taiwan amounts to a National Missile Defence system for them? In the eyes of the US, a theatre-wide defence might cover part of one's territory, but in the eyes of a small country it provides complete protection. This is where perhaps the distinction needs to be made.

Dr. Fergusson

Yes. And it has implications for the treaty process and the legal regime and the politics behind it. I would suggest that the Japanese and the Chinese and all the others who talk about the ABM treaty should start considering becoming members of the treaty because they are not bound by it. No matter what they say, they are not legally bound by that treaty, only Russia and the United States are.

Captain Andrew Godefroy, Directorate of Space Development, DND

Dr. Fergusson, you brought forth the key point that there seems to be an aggressive agenda by Europe to dissuade Canada from participating in the National Missile Defence process. I was wondering if you could elaborate a little more on some of the particular preventive diplomacy that Europe is carrying out against Canada, if they are going to that length yet, and what sort of impact that may have on our own decision-making process.

Dr. Fergusson

I may have misspoken, or you may have misinterpreted me. The Europeans are not trying to influence Canada whatsoever about this. I think much of the debate in Europe — the opposition in Europe — is intended more for domestic political consumption in Europe than trying to influence the debate in the United States. I would agree with you that, in Canada, the government will interpret what is in the press or speeches by the Foreign Minister of Germany or by the President of France, and will take that as a way to rationalize or legitimize Canadian concerns or Canadian opposition. They will take European views as meaningful and something that should be considered at the end of the day in Canadian policy. These views really should have no bearing on Canada at all, except at the margin in terms of whether NMD is a future threat to the Alliance, and I don't think it is.

Colonel Alain Pellerin, Conference of Defence Associations (CDA)

Just a follow up to the comment that Dr. Fergusson was making about the distinction between TMD and National Missile Defence. Lets just talk about a missile defence that would essentially try to destroy missiles in their boost phases, or the area around the boost phase, as opposed to incoming missiles over the territory of North America in their terminal phase. How credible would that be to Washington as a missile defence – call it TMD, NMD or both? Would that be a credible system, and if so then it would get around the difficulty with the ABM?

Dr. Fergusson

It goes back to the way that we've arbitrarily, for clearly political reasons, made these categories. I still argue that, today at least, they are arbitrary categories, but I understand the political importance of them. The United States is developing National Missile Defence but I think that, even though they talk about theatre missile defence for forward-deployed forces, questions remain about whether this type of defence will suffice. For an ICBM, depending upon the flight timing, the boost phase is estimated between two-and-a-half to five minutes. Do you have the satellite-based systems, the command and control, to be able to respond and fire a missile fast enough? But the point is that that in fact when TMD systems do get forward deployed they will become the first layer of a much bigger missile defence system. I think we have to recognize that National Missile Defence is important today for that ground-based, mid-course intercept capability. But you cannot arbitrarily rip out theatre missile defence, particularly upper-tier, and lower tier as well, because when they are forward deployed, they are part of a layer. But what's missing in the layer (and for any of you that suddenly think aha! it's SDI) is that there is no interest, very little support, even among the hard-line Republicans, to go to the exotic spaced-based interceptors, so that's not going to happen. Then of course when you talk about forward-deployed systems, depending on where they're located, what forces do they threaten? The general argument is that they don't threaten Russian strategic forces because you're not going to be able to put a naval task force in the Arctic Ocean to take a shot early on — unless global warming melts the ice caps! I guess at the end of the day part of the problem is that we're still living in a legacy of old Cold War categories, which in fact make it very difficult to understand exactly what this system is and where this is really going.

Mohammed Khan, former research associate, Arms Control and Disarmament Centre, University of Illinois

My question is regarding non-proliferation. How would national defence systems in Canada, the United States or Europe, affect the Missile Technology Control Regime (MTCR)? There is a lot of preaching from the west to South-East Asia, South Asia and the Middle East about non-proliferation, but we are developing something that goes against the MTCR rules, and the proliferation of weapons of mass destruction could result.

Dr. Henderson

The obvious point is that North Korea has been selling medium-range missiles for quite some time, whether it's the entire missile, or parts of it, or just missile technology. It appears almost certain that China has been doing much the same for Pakistan. The MTCR regime has not stopped this, though the US works very hard to try to limit it. For example, there was the case of the — I believe it was Chinese — vessel that the US was tracking by satellite as it traveled around South Asia. They hoped to find missile parts on it but, even with their capability, which has to be literally state-of-the-art by world standards, it's a very difficult proposition. It is one thing to have a regime which everybody or most countries have signed, but it's another thing to actually enforce it.

Dr. Fergusson

Let me give you two answers. First of all, the deployment of missile defences does not in any way violate the MTCR regime, which is a non-proliferation regime for ballistic or cruise missiles, not missile defences. I agree with the problems of enforcement and other weaknesses about the regime, not least of all the issue between distinguishing between legitimate, commercially-driven and scientifically-driven space launch vehicles and ballistic missiles. That's a real big problem that no one really wants to talk about. But I don't see NMD as a problem for MTCR. We think of the ABM treaty as a symbol that has really very little to do with strategic stability. It is an important symbol and there are a variety of reasons why states will continue to attempt to stumble along and use it as one of the many barriers [to proliferation]. It is a part of a bigger picture: the non-proliferation regime.

Let me give you the second answer. I think you raise an even more important point that puzzles me. One thinks about missile defence and its impact on proliferation largely in old Cold War terms — ie. it will generate arms races, it will drive states to acquire ballistic missiles, etc. What puzzles me, however, is why we don't think in terms of the limited investment and the high-technology demands for small underdeveloped (or relatively underdeveloped) countries, if they wish to invest in ballistic missiles. Why don't we think that missile defences, if deployed, will alter their calculus about whether or not they should invest in these weapons. That's not an answer that may channel their military investments into other areas which the West doesn't like, but it may be a non-proliferation tool itself. I think if we start to think in non-proliferation terms, we can start to have a different idea about typologies of missile defences — deployment patterns which may promote non-proliferation, but in other situations may be negative.

Let me conclude with one last point. Look at the case of Taiwan and ask what the West's preferences are. Do we want a Taiwan that develops missile defence, or would be prefer (and there is a very quiet debate going on about this in Taiwan) a Taiwan that decides not to bother with missile defence, and instead acquires offensive ballistic missiles and perhaps goes down the nuclear path. My view on that, if these are the options that people are thinking about (and some are) in Taiwan, then the answer is, it's better to stay in the defence realm than create incentives for them to go offensive to deal with China.

Dr. Henderson

On the Taiwan issue, we are talking about an offensive capability. Last December, the Kuomintang (KMT) Party Vice-President made the comment that Taiwan needed a more credible second-strike capability to deter China. This second-strike capability was basically the air force, stand-off weapons and so on. The defence minister who has now become the Premiere said categorically the next day that this was not policy and they were not taking an offensive approach; they were only talking about defence of Taiwan. So they were very public about not contemplating an offensive deterrent capability. But internally the KMT government may very well have been having that debate.

THE CASE AGAINST NATIONAL MISSILE DEFENCE: A CANADIAN PERSPECTIVE

Bill Robinson

I was a little worried that Jim Fergusson would convince me this morning that National Missile Defence (NMD) was a good idea, but fortunately that didn't happen so I'll be able to make my presentation to you.

Missile defence is often promoted as a kind of technological question — if the technology works we should deploy it, if it doesn't we shouldn't. Technology is an important aspect — because if it doesn't work, and there are serious doubts that it will, that is obviously a major problem — but it is not the fundamental question. The fundamental question is, what effect would missile defence have on our security, especially if it works?

The first point I want to make is that the missile defence plan is likely to increase, not reduce, the threat posed by weapons of mass destruction (primarily nuclear but not exclusively) to Canada and to global security in general. I believe that Canada needs to address those security consequences. Certain proponents of missile defence suggest that the only decision for Canada is how it will affect Canada-US relations, so we should not even consider its security consequences. I would argue that that is not the position that Canada should take. We need to carefully look at the effects of NMD on our relations with, and the stability of global relations with, Russia, the effects on China, the question of proliferation, and then what missile defence might have to say about the so-called "rogue" threat. I argue that non-participation is the best choice for Canada and that we should instead propose constructive alternatives as a means of

Bill Robinson is Program Associate at Project Ploughshares, Waterloo, ON.

addressing the threat that weapons of mass destruction (WMD) pose to the world.

WMD Threat – Russia

Russia is, I think, something that we do need to take very seriously. Russia continues to place a very high priority on maintaining a nuclear deterrent even though it cannot afford to maintain the size of force that it has now. There was a discussion this morning about the distinction between strategic and tactical missile defence. I think the important distinction to think about here is the question of what happens when you deploy a missile defence and you already have a strong offensive nuclear force. When those two things are in combination, it is a very different situation. A strategic missile defence of Taiwan, for example, doesn't have the same kind of effect that you get when you combine missile defence and offensive nuclear capabilities. This is what we're concerned about with the United States deploying missile defence and what effect it might have on the relationship with Russia.

Missile defence does pose a potential threat to the Russia deterrent, despite what the Minister of National Defence said this morning. There are two reasons for saying that. The first is, you have to look at the combined offence capabilities and defence capabilities. What the Russians are going to be worried about is not that they might lose the ability to conduct a first strike against the United States; they're going to be worried about whether or not they have a deterrent force that could survive attack by the United States and still retaliate. Now, I don't think they need that capability, but they don't listen to me. They are putting a lot of effort into maintaining that capability with money they don't have. They do take it seriously and they will attempt to maintain it. I don't have a lot of time to go into this in detail, but let me just say that America's offensive capability right now is very high. That doesn't mean that anyone here or in Russia thinks that there is going to be a first strike by the United States against Russia, but the capability is there. Right now, we're talking about perhaps 3,000 to 4,000 ICBM-based warheads that the US could deliver to a target base of about 800 targets in Russia, plus one or two submarine-launched ballistic missiles (SLBMs) at sea. When we're talking about Strategic Arms Reduction Treaty (START) agreements, even with START III, we could be talking about 800 to 1,000 hard target-killing warheads against a target base of 400-500 targets, plus the warheads of one missile submarine at sea. So the threat right now, and in the future based on current arms control plans, would, in the worst-case analysis, leave the Russians with some tens of warheads survivable from a first strike. And that would be the kind of thing that they would be talking about — how would that get through a missile defence system? So even the initial limited missile defence system poses some threat to that Russian second-strike deterrent capability.

Now the Russians have advanced counter-measure techniques, and so, in practical terms, a limited missile defence probably would not stop them; certainly the United States could not count on stopping them. But nonetheless it would start to put them in a position of not having a very credible deterrent. But the second thing the Russians really have to worry about is that there would be extreme potential for rapid expansion of such a missile defence system. They do have to worry about that because there are voices in the United States that want to do that. You only have to read Space Command's documents (which they publish to the public, on the web) to know that there is interest in a lot more advanced strategic defences than simply limited National Missile Defence. That interest extends into the political system, as well as the military. It hasn't won the day, but it is a factor, and the Russians have to be concerned about it. If the US deploys this limited missile defence system, they will have deployed the basic sensor and command and control infrastructure for a much larger system — meaning radars, space-based sensors, and the command and control system. Those are the long-lead items to building a much more extensive missile defence system. Once you've built those for a small system, you have created a potential expansion capability that the Russians must take seriously. Secondly, of course, there are problems like Navy Theatre-Wide (NTW) missile defence systems, which could be netted into the NMD system and cause it to rapidly expand. There are proposals to do that very thing.

There are many possible responses for the Russians. Withdrawal from existing arms control agreements is certainly a possibility, and that would tend to lessen our security. The START II was recently ratified by the Duma, but explicitly with the provision that they could withdraw from it if the Americans deploy a missile defence system. Also likely is the retention of larger nuclear forces — larger ones than they would otherwise have had. The number of forces is declining for economic reasons in Russia, but they would very likely keep forces in place that they would otherwise have retired and stretch their lifetimes. As well, they could MIRV (multiple independent reentry vehicle — in other words, put several warheads on one missile) systems that are not currently planned to be MIRVed. So we're talking about more warheads than there would otherwise have been. Continued operation on high alert is also very likely, I think, if the US proceeds along the missile defence road. And this is perhaps the singular greatest threat of nuclear attack to the world right now: the danger that high-alert operations will result in some kind of accidental war. Finally, a renewed arms race is possible over the longer term. It is not likely in the short term, if only for economic reasons, but we all know that Germany was an economic basket case in the 1920s and economic circumstances do change. We have to think about longer-term relationships.

It is possible that there will be an ABM deal. That would mitigate some of these problems. It would be a political deal, however, the military people over in Russia would not be happy with it at all and I think there are some serious questions about it. There are questions about whether you could get it ratified in the US Senate, there are questions about whether you could get it ratified in the Duma, there are questions about whether it would endure in the United States or in Russia against the pressures to back away from it or, in the United States, to deploy a larger system. There's still the problem of China, which I will be talking about in a minute. And you would still probably see a lot of these things — more warheads than otherwise, higher alert operations than otherwise — and so a greater threat of nuclear war, an increased risk of accidental or inadvertent war than there would otherwise be, and an increased problem in the US' relationship with Russia that could mean trouble further down the road.

WMD Threat — China

With respect to China, the situation is rather similar, so I won't make the arguments in great detail. China now has a very minimal nuclear deterrent: about 20 to 24 ICBMs capable of hitting North America. They are not fueled, we are told, and, according to some sources, including the intelligence community, they do not have their warheads mated. So there is absolutely no risk of accidental war from this arsenal at this time. But, the Chinese are certainly looking at modernizing that arsenal and one of the reasons for this is the pressure from the potential deployment of missile defence.

US missile defence obviously does pose a very serious threat to a capability of 20 to 24 missiles — we're talking about 100 interceptors initially, and then the possibility of a larger systems. A US-Russia ABM deal would obviously not resolve this problem at all, and there are several possible responses that China could make.

The deployment of larger, more capable nuclear forces is quite likely. The Chinese are already starting to look at doing that. They have had the potential to do it for decades but, as yet, have not gone beyond a minimal force. What may drive them to deploy this greater force would be missile defence.

A change to higher alert operations is a possibility, though not a certainty. Asymmetrical response has also been raised as a possible Chinese response. Their military writings talk about counter-space operations that would be threatening to the sensor systems in space as well as to commercial operations in space. One possible way for China to respond would be to up the ante and say that if there is going to be movement of this kind of system into space, space is not going to a sanctuary and commercial operations will be at threat in the event of war. We're talking about trillions of dollars in investment up there, and the idea of upping that ante would be try and get commercial interests onside against the deployment of such things. Whether it'll happen or not, we'll have to see.

The probable result, however, is a much increased risk of accidental or nuclear war because you're going from zero risk to at least some risk. Again, there will be increased tensions in the relationship. The long-term relationship with China is, of course, very important for the security of all of us. This is not likely to be the make or break issue, but it's one more way in which we might end up going down the wrong road in our relationship with China.

WMD Threat – Proliferation

Vertical

On the broader proliferation question, if you get Russian and Chinese responses of this nature, you could see a cascade of reactions. These could include possible further US reactions to what Russia and China have done, and British and French reactions to Russian moves in particular. In response to a larger Chinese nuclear force, we could be seeing a larger Indian response, and in turn a Pakistani response to Indian initiatives. These are possibilities.

Horizontal

On the horizontal proliferation scale, if we see these vertical reactions, then we are looking at halting, or even reversing the arms control progress of the past decades. So we see the potential for the further erosion of the Non-Proliferation Treaty (NPT), with the possibility that some countries will themselves chose to move down the nuclear or weapons of mass destruction road. Now, I don't put this down as a probable result, unlike the other things, I would say this is more of a worst case scenario, something to consider. But there is a danger of tipping off a set of actions and reactions that would lead to wider spread of nuclear capability and therefore increased risk of nuclear use.

WMD Threat — "Rogue" States

Against all of these reasons for *not* fielding the US NMD system, we have the reason *for* deploying such as system, which is principally given as the danger from rogue states — namely North Korea, Iran and Iraq. The first point is, of course, that the missile capability the Americans are worried about does not currently exist. It's a potential. The US national intelligence community has a rather good report out on the potential technological development of such capabilities, or whether they could acquire them from other countries. But one of the things it notes is that it does not at all address potential for political or economic changes in these countries. And so it is not a prediction of what is likely to happen, it is purely an assessment of technological capabilities; whether they *might* be able to deploy missile defences. And that's relevant to alternative approaches to managing the threat because we're looking at a moderating trend in Iran that may very well continue and could be encouraged. We're looking at the fact that in North Korea there is a freeze [on the nuclear weapons program], and of course Iraq remains under very heavy military sanctions. So that is also a fairly distant threat, I would argue.

There is certainly potential then to bring about changes that would not lead to the actual existence of this so-called missile threat. Nonetheless, a weapons of mass destruction capability does exist. Here we're really talking about chemical weapons, and possibly biological weapons. North Korea is close to having a nuclear capability and may have enough material for one bomb, or two if it's a very sophisticated bomb (which it's highly unlikely to be). So there is a weapons of mass destruction capability, but this is a different problem — this is not a missile capability, this is a weapons of mass destruction capability. It exists now, and if the North Koreans wanted to deliver such weapons to the United States, they could do it now. They wouldn't do it by ballistic missile.

Nonetheless, if a missile capability does develop, would a National

Missile Defence deal with that problem of an attack using weapons of mass destruction? Countermeasures could, very likely, defeat the NMD system. There have been arguments back and forth about this. At the very least such offensive counter-measures would force the United States to deploy a larger and more sophisticated system in response to them, and this would bring us back to the problem of Russia and China very quickly. In the case of biological or chemical weapons, submunitions are the best delivery system. Now, apparently the technology for submunitions is not that difficult (I'm not a techie in that sense) but the important point is that submunition delivery is entirely impossible to intercept using the National Missile Defence technology. They could stop one submunition perhaps, but there would be tens or hundreds of these things from each missile. So the system would be entirely incapable of dealing with such a threat. The other important point (and I think this is a vitally important point) is that there are other delivery methods available, which I already alluded to.

If rogue states really want to deliver such weapons, ballistic missiles are not necessary to do it. This once again comes from a US National Intelligence Assessment. You can get it on the CIA website, the unclassified version. I recommend you read it. It lists the following as suggested alternative delivery methods, which would be well within the capability of such countries. One option is forward-based short-range ballistic missiles (SRBMs), which could be a Scud-style system just mounted on the deck of a ship. Another possibility is land attack cruise missiles. Finally, even more simply, just put one on a ship, or in a commercial aircraft baggage bay and fly it into an airport, or smuggle it in otherwise, or even prepare it inside the United States itself. And this is not me saying this, remember, it's the CIA.

I have already listed several advantages such systems have over ICBMs. Such modes will be generally less expensive, more reliable, more accurate, and more effective for biological weapons dissemination. You could potentially mask the source of the attack (which is useful if you care to survive much longer after it's occurred), and of course it avoids missile defences. So the probable result of an NMD deployment would essentially be a Maginot Line. It may be true in baseball movies that if you deploy it, they will come, if you build it, they will come. In defence, typically, if you build it, they will go around it. And that's exactly the likely thing that would happen if the US deployed such a system. So if it worked, missile defence would be far more likely to affect the means of attack than the ability to attack, if we assume there was in fact an interest in attacking.

WMD Threat – Balancing the Risks

There is no risk-free approach to dealing with these problems, but you have to balance the risks that are there based on what you think is the most likely result. My argument would be that the potential benefits of missile defence do not in any way justify the potential risks from such a program. It is extremely unlikely to be able to stop an attack from a determined rogue state that actually wants to get to the target and decides to choose a method that will do it. And, in my view, it is quite unlikely that such a state would in fact choose to make such an attack and commit suicide. They do have the capability to deliver such weapons now. They have not done so, probably because they want to live longer.

If you were to get a robust US-Russian-Chinese consensus on the desirability and nature of missile defences (and by robust I don't mean a simple deal bullied out of Putin for short-term economic benefits) then most of the ill-effects of a such a system deployment might be mitigated and then we might be able to talk about whether it's really worth spending the money for very minimal capability against a very minimal threat. But until you have that horse before the cart, it is madness to deploy a missile defence.

Yes, a short-range regional boost phase system that would, for example, be capable only against North Korea and not have significant capabilities against China (if such a thing could be designed and agreed upon with the Chinese) might be worth exploring, if you felt you needed that kind of system, but this is not at all what is on the table right now. However, it is getting increased attention in the United States. I know, for example, that Rep. Kurt Weldon, one of the big supporters of missile defence, is quite interested in that approach and there is some suggestion that the Russians may also have some interest in that possibility. If the US insists upon deploying something, that would be the least damaging way to do it. Nonetheless, it is not on the table right now and if we were to support National Missile Defence, we would not be supporting that.

We do need to address the security consequences of such things. There is a claim that missile defence deployment is a foregone conclusion, but there are all kinds of aspects to its nature. There is the question of when the decision is made, but there is also what type of system is deployed and how does it evolve over time. This is not a single decision. These are several decisions that will be made over many years. For example, we have the case of the Sentinel system authorized for deployment in

1967, which later became Safeguard, a completely different system, which was deployed in the early 70s. The ABM treaty was then subsequently developed and the Safeguard system was later retired. A simple deployment decision, such as was made in 1967, is far from the end of the issue.

So, we should not accept the argument that missile defence deployment is a forgone conclusion and Canada can do nothing except decide how it's going to affect Canada-US relations, and whether we're on board. We should not abdicate responsibility for our own security. Missile defence does threaten our security and there is opposition rising within the United States, it's slow but coming. Allied views are also important. I think you can speculate on how serious they are, but the point I want to make is that in fact the current NMD system does require deployment of some material in some allied states — not in Canada but in the UK, in Denmark and ultimately in South Korea if they agree, so in such cases the views of allies are very important on whether that system can in fact be deployed.

Non-Participation

Non-participation is the best choice for Canada. Our influence is certainly limited but nonetheless it is still important, and that is why the United States would in fact like to see our decision come down in favour of missile defence instead of against it. I find it ironic that the Pentagon is interested in Canadian soft power, because that's what they're asking us to contribute to this system, not money or geography. Canadian soft power is obviously of some interest to them, and it is also of interest to other people.

Participating in NMD wouldn't increase our influence. We're not bringing anything to the table that is going to cause them to change their plans based on us being on board and threatening to withdraw later if they don't modify the system or something like that. And once we have given our support, we will have given the one thing we can give.

Non-participation would not threaten Canada-US relations. I don't have time to go into this, but I'm sure it will come up. We have a much broader relationship with the US than this single issue, as was mentioned this morning. The US does not need Canadian participation, although some elements would like it. We have frequent disagreements on many issues, so we are not talking about the end of Canada-US relations here, as is sometimes implied.

The NORAD relationship could continue too. I was recently in Colorado Springs and listened to the NORAD briefing. They forget that such a system was deployed in the past; there was in fact a ballistic missile defence centre in the NORAD command centre in the 1970s. It was US-only, yet NORAD continued to operate with US-Canadian roles as well. These things can happen. US-Canadian and US-only roles do interact at NORAD at all times. They do right now and they could in the future. Alternative Canadian contributions are possible.

Constructive Alternatives

We should recognize that weapons of mass destruction do pose a threat to our security. Missiles are a small element of that problem. The US and Russian nuclear arsenals are by far the primary threat, and if anything went seriously wrong with those it would be the end of our history. The secondary nuclear powers are the next level of threat, and nuclear or other weapons of mass destruction proliferants come way down the list, although some people may argue they are somewhat more likely to use their weapons.

We should actively support alternative approaches to dealing with these problems. These would include, notably, measures to mitigate the threat posed by the US and Russian arsenals: deeper reductions in the context of a preserved ABM Treaty, reduction of counterforce capabilities, de-alerting/de-mating measures, co-operative early warning/monitoring measures. These alternative courses of action would deal with much of what I've just talked about and some of these things are very practical for even small states to help contribute to. The Russians have a very big problem with their early warning system — it is falling apart — and that means that they do not know for certain when they are *not* under attack. It is very important for us to have them know when they are not under attack. This is vital to our security. It would take a few hundred million dollars — US$600-million is one estimate — to put up the Russian early warning satellites that they have already built but cannot afford to launch. So that's the kind of thing that even small states in cooperation with each other could help to do that would in fact make everybody, including the United States, a lot safer.

I alluded to negotiating and engagement with "rogue" states when I was talking about the various programs to freeze the testing programs or to deal with moderating influences in Iran and so forth. This approach, too, is worth pursuing.

Preservation and extension of global arms control regimes and finally cooperative security measures are also worthwhile approaches. Weapons of mass destruction capabilities exist in industrial society at this point. Even if you could eliminate them all, and I believe that you can move toward nuclear abolition, for example, you will not eliminate the knowledge to create those weapons. That knowledge will be there and so a certain level of vulnerability will be there for the rest of human history. The way to manage that vulnerability is to move away from adversarial relations. It's a long-term thing, it's not guaranteed to succeed but it's the only thing that *will* succeed in the long term. It should certainly be one of our approaches too.

CANADA AND NATIONAL MISSILE DEFENCE : A NORAD PERSPECTIVE

LGen (Retd) Robert W. Morton

Introduction

My task is to give a NORAD operator's view on the subject and title of today's seminar. To do that I'd like to share recollections and personal views that I gained over many years of NORAD duty during the Cold War, the Persian Gulf war a decade ago, and gleaned from international developments of recent years.

I just had the opportunity to refresh my memory of what goes on at the NORAD command centre inside Cheyenne Mountain a few weeks ago at the invitation of General MacDonald, the current Deputy Commander-in-Chief (DCINC), and it's a beehive of activity, a high tech masterpiece. Canadians are integrated intimately throughout the staff of the complex.

I'd like, first, to lead up to the issue of National Missile Defence (NMD) by taking a look at Canada/US aerospace defence cooperation over the years, including how it got started; changes in strategy and equipment instituted as threats evolved from aircraft to missiles, ballistic and cruise; how NORAD's mission adapted along the way; new circumstances as the Cold War faded into history; and, why new political and technological realities have led inevitably to a US interest in ballistic missile defence.

I will then narrow the focus to the theme of the seminar and answer the following questions:

LGen (Retd) Robert W. Morton is former Deputy Commander-in-Chief, NORAD.

- Should NMD become a NORAD mission and be tied into the NORAD Command and Control structure? The short answer is yes.
- Does it fit? The short answer is yes.
- What are implications for Canada and NORAD if the US decides to deploy and Canada is not aboard? The short answer is bad.
- What connections exist between NMD and other Canada-US defence and security issues? The short answer is that they are many-faceted and that all are vulnerable.

The Issue

During the Cold War, any attack against North America would probably have come from the former Soviet Union. Now, according to US intelligence assessments, due to changed politics and advances in technologies of all kinds, potential sources of missile attacks have widened. States with negative views of the US or its policies will soon be capable of a direct nuclear, biological or chemical attack against the continental United States.

The US is concerned that its strategy of deterrence — which could include retaliation in kind against rogue states — might not restrain reckless actions against the US. It is, therefore, investigating missile defense technologies that not only can deter but also can defend against this new military capability, should it ever be unleashed. If the technological search is successful, the US is contemplating deployment of a limited-capability defence against ballistic missile attack. Given the history of our continental defence cooperation, the US is hopeful of Canada's support and co-operation.

I agree with Jim Fergusson's point this morning in answer to the last question, that the presence of the NMD can have a major deterrent impact, even to the point of perhaps persuading these rogue states and dictators that it's not worth the investment to proceed with an ICBM capability, given the fact of an NMD presence.

The US has not issued a formal invitation for Canada to participate; but neither has Canada shown eagerness to climb aboard, although some research and development (R&D) into related technologies has been conducted. So the dance is underway, but without much music. Canada's diminished enthusiasm for any defence measure or defence program is evident in this hesitancy, and that too is stalling progress.

I'd characterize the background lyrics like this: From Ottawa: *don't ask the question because it might cost money*; from Washington: *don't ask the question if the answer may be wrong*! Another reason for Canada's hesitancy is, I believe, that NMD represents a change in US strategy from purely deterrence to one that includes some defence — a blend needed to meet new and different threats from those faced in Cold War. That change, sensed by many Americans as necessary for future US security, is not widely understood in Canada.

There's an irony in this because many Canadians abhor the Cold War strategy of deterrence, in spite of the fact it worked successfully for forty years. Its doctrine of an eye-for-an-eye — Mutually Assured Destruction (MAD) — has surely the most descriptive acronym in the history of human conflict. But the time for that doctrine has passed; it is no longer a morally or politically acceptable doctrine. Thankfully, it is no longer necessary.

But, as our US friends have done, we too must ask ourselves: what doctrine or strategy should take its place? What measures contribute to the avoidance of conflict in these times? What new policies or capabilities does the new international environment demand?

My many years at ground zero in command and control (C2) centers, thinking about these things while keeping watch for new test launches, convinced me that wishing away these problems is not of much value. Nor will peace be enhanced by political demands for non-proliferation, scholarly treatises on arms control, or paper treaties; at least, not without verification means, and not without the framework of a workable strategy.

Instead, collectively we must possess, demonstrate means, and show conviction to exploit military strength if and when that is needed. And that doesn't mean to start design work on a defensive system when a hostile launch is detected somewhere. In the real world, peacemakers have never been dreamers who for the maintenance of peace rely on human goodness, or the good faith of dictators. Peacemakers are those whose strategy discourages, deters, or defeats aggressors. Tyrants understand that. In democracies, it's a mystery that we don't.

Concerns

What are Canada's concerns about NMD? One is the potential impact on the Anti-Ballistic Missile (ABM) Treaty, an arms control breakthrough from 1972, that helped stabilize the balance of nuclear power. It was essentially a 'firebreak' in the Cold War to ensure that neither superpower could develop a sense of invulnerability and consider a disarming first strike against the other. Like all arms control achievements it remains important, but its main value was derived in the MAD era where it applied to a different set of problems than the new ones faced today. The ABM Treaty was a key stabilizing part of an earlier nuclear strategy; negotiations are now underway between the two signatories to seek accommodation on amendments that would permit the US to deploy NMD. Russian actions this past week hint at some progress in that direction.

The "rogue state" threat introduces a problem that did not exist in 1972 and is, in reality, a concern for both the US and Russia. This recent action by the Russian Duma of finally approving START II may signal that they see merit in some accommodation with the US, not yet announced, on ABM Treaty amendments.

Another concern should be Canadian security. It's understandable that Canada would not wish to see any unraveling or abrogation of the ABM Treaty. But the potential direct threat to Canadian territory should be at least an equal worry. Many would argue it is a bigger worry. A missile aimed at major US population centres from, say, the Middle East or East Asia could, with a tiny error in direction or distance, end up falling short and landing in Canada. So, whether we are involved as a partner in a missile defence system or not, we could be an unintended target. We should throw away our flat mercator maps and start looking at a globe of the earth, pairing random launch points abroad with possible targets in the Continental United States (CONUS), to understand this unique Canadian problem.

History

That space-age fact of physics and geography reminds us that the interdependence of Canada and the US for defence against armed attack is, at root, a function of geography. In 1938, at the opening of the Thousand Island bridge across the St. Lawrence, and with the threat of war looming in Europe, President Roosevelt said in a speech at Queen's University in Kingston that the "US would not stand idly by if Canada were threatened by any other empire."

Several days later Prime Minister Mackenzie King responded, acknowledging Canada's obligations "as a good and friendly neighbour," and assured his counterpart that Canada would "at our own instance, make our country as immune from attack as we can reasonably be expected to make it" and that, "should the occasion ever arise, enemy forces should not be able to pursue their way, either by land, sea, or air to the United States, across Canadian territory."

In 1938 the PM had no need to include 'space' in his security assurances along with land, sea and air. But the intent of his assurance — a willingness to take responsibility for security of northern approaches to the US — was both honorable and clear. Should Canada not still honor the pledge?

NORAD Command Formation — The Beginning

Twenty years later, in 1958, at the dawn of the space age, and in a new geostrategic era, those pre-World War II exchanges on sharing defence were further reinforced by the signing of the NORAD Agreement, creating the combined US-Canada command, with some of both nations' aircraft, ground radar, and personnel assigned to NORAD duty.

Now, the 42-year history of NORAD is a testimonial to the merits of this co-operative arrangement as judged by successive governments in both countries. The first agreement charged the command with continental air defence against long-range Soviet bombers — defence, not deterrence. That required hundreds of radars, thousands of fighter-interceptor aircraft and, for a brief period, surface-to-air missiles and anti-aircraft guns. Command and control boundaries straddled the border, giving Canadian commanders operational control over parts of the USA, and US commanders control over parts of Canada.

In the 1960s, ICBMs supplanted bombers as the major Soviet threat to North America. Since no adequate defence against missile attack was then possible, the strategy shifted from defence to deterrence, and the resources assigned to air defence were reduced significantly. NORAD's contribution to continental defence was changed by mutual agreement to include warning and characterization of nuclear attack. New sensors to give warning of missile attack were developed and deployed, paid for entirely by the USA. Information derived from these sensors was shared with Canada in accordance with the terms of the agreement. The US paid for 60% of Canada's North Warning System and for 50% of Canada's Forward Operating Locations. So the US taxpayer has footed large portions of the bill — 100% of US systems, 40 to 60% of Canadian systems — and we share the benefits from all of their capital investment, along with all the benefits we derive from things that are in Canada.

In 1975, a renewal of the NORAD agreement codified changes in command objectives. The mission statement was modified to include the maintenance of airspace sovereignty as a specific task. Contribution to deterrence by providing warning and attack characterization was retained, as was the original task: response to air attack. At the next renewal of the treaty, command and control boundaries were re-aligned to coincide with national boundaries, resulting in three NORAD Regions: Alaska, Canada, and the CONUS. These remain unchanged to this day.

At the seventh renewal in 1991, NORAD's role in counter-drug activities was added, indicating that the air sovereignty mission was to include surveillance and monitoring of aircraft suspected of smuggling illegal drugs. NORAD still has this task, cooperating with law enforcement agencies in both countries.

The most recent renewal in 1996 assigned primary missions as aerospace warning and aerospace control for North America. Aerospace warning was defined as monitoring of man-made objects in space and detection, validation, and warning of attack against North America by aircraft, missiles, or space vehicles, utilizing mutual support arrangements of other commands. This mission includes monitoring of global aerospace activities and related developments (current count: 8,200 man-made objects in earth orbit, of 26,000 launched). Aerospace control includes providing surveillance and control of the airspace of each of our nations.

The 1996 exchange of notes highlighted changes in the geostrategic environment that altered the Cold War threat. START treaties and other arms control initiatives showed promise of deep cuts in strategic ballistic missile forces. And yet the notes acknowledged that large residual nuclear arsenals will still exist after programmed treaty reductions are made. They acknowledged that proliferation of weapons of mass destruction and delivery systems has emerged as a major security challenge, and that the significance of space has grown as an increasingly important component of most traditional military activities.

Thus, over the years, the missions of NORAD have changed to meet different threats and priorities. At each renewal, the opportunity existed not only to amend missions, but also to examine the continuing relevance of a shared aerospace defence structure.

NORAD Today – Sensible Missions

Aerospace Control

Given Canada/US geographical links, a common interest in aerospace sovereignty, significant cost-shared investments in a modern integrated radar surveillance network, and a history of successful aerospace defence cooperation, it would appear that continuing to share responsibility in airspace control makes good sense, militarily and economically. Assisting law enforcement to interdict aerial drug smuggling enjoys wide public support.

Air Attack Warning and Air Defence

While much discussion of late is of concern about ballistic weapons, cruise missiles and long-range bomber aircraft remain in inventories of foreign states as components of their strategic arsenals. These too are being modernized and must be considered in NORAD's aerospace control, attack warning, and air defence mandates.

Aerospace Warning

In my judgement, this is the key mission that is carried out in the Cheyenne Mountain complex. The ballistic missile attack warning and characterization mission has been performed for both countries by NORAD since the 1960s and will remain, without question, a key component of United States security policy. Nuclear warheads and operational ballistic missiles owned by other states on land and at sea guarantee that. The warning mission will exist for the USA whether Canada chooses to stay involved in the mission or not. If not performed in a binational forum such as NORAD on behalf of both countries, then the mission will probably be switched to the collocated Unified Space Command, presumably with a mission of attack warning for the USA only.

Withdrawal (or being excluded) from this key part of the aerospace mission would be a serious loss to Canada's security interests. Canadians must bear in mind that the military power to destroy this country still exists in the hands of other states and will remain so well into this century – even after the START draw-down has been completed. Moreover, possession of ballistic missile technologies and other powerful weapons has expanded to new states. The areas of concern and observation for missile launch detection now extend beyond the ICBM fields and mobile launch points in the former Soviet Union or its ballistic missile submarine patrol areas.

Theatre Warning

Ten years ago, the warning of launch of Iraqi SCUD missiles, and the resultant opportunity to seek shelter from unseen weapons launched hundreds of kilometers away, raised the consciousness of many Canadians in the Persian Gulf of unexpected threats to their safety. SCUDs and other ballistic types are widely dispersed and might be faced by Canadians in the future across a spectrum of conflict from peace operations to coalition warfare. Having direct access to the NORAD attack warning system is therefore highly desirable for Canada.

Peace Operations Warning

The ability to give clear, unambiguous warning of missile attack will remain an important military mission at home and, increasingly, abroad. Canada's love affair with peacekeeping and willingness to commit military personnel to dangerous duty in foreign lands raises questions of their safety in this era of missile proliferation. Short and medium range missile systems will threaten our peacekeepers abroad. They face quite enough danger from sources they see; NORAD helps with those they can't!

NORAD Mission Today – Equipment and Process

I could spend my entire time allocation on a description of fielded and spaceborne systems that allow NORAD to accomplish its missions. Were I to do that I would fail my task. Thus, I will simply name the systems; they have terms you will find familiar. I invite questions later if you desire more explanation.

Here are the main systems that support NORAD's missions:

- Defense Support Program (DSP) — even the acronym used to be classified, now everyone knows about it. It became public knowledge during the Persian Gulf War because everyone knew the Scuds were being detected. How were they being detected? Well, they were being detected by the Defense Support Program's constellation of satellites.
- Missile Warning — Ground Radars — Ballistic Missile Early

Warning System (BMEWS) — PAVE PAWS
- Atmospheric Radars — North Warning Systems (NWS) — Coastal Radars
- Aerostats
- Airborne Warning and Control System (AWACS)
- Fighters
- Alert Sites and Forward Operating Locations (FOLs)
- Airlift
- Command, Control, Communications, Computers, Intelligence
- Cheyenne Mountain Complex — Regional Command Centre (RCC) — SAOC

The point is, it's a very complex system that has to be integrated to make it work. You take away one or two pieces of that and the puzzle doesn't make any sense.

Communications are critical. Time-sensitive or warning communications uplinks are made simultaneously to the National Military Command Centre (NMCC) in Washington and the National Defence Operations Centre (NDOC) in Ottawa. From these centers, national links reach out to commands, units, and formations worldwide.

Aerospace control works on the principle of centralized control/decentralized execution because of the very large number of international flights entering North America. For example, approximately 7000 airliner flights enter North American airspace from overseas each day, or roughly 2.5 million flights a year. All must be identified. This is done at the RCC/SAOC levels, with unknown tracks or high interest tracks forwarded on to Cheyenne Mountain.

The fusion of data — either from ballistic missile early warning radars, DSP satellites, aerostats on the Mexican-US border, or the North Warning Systems in Canada — is a very complicated process. It's not something that you can piecemeal apart and segregate on basis of a perceived need to segregate responsibilities. Success or failure of the mission rests in the ability to combine reliable data from all sensors — ground, air, and space — display the relevant and verified data in useable form for human interpretation and assessment, and communicate appropriate actions to subscribers. There is no time for error. For example, the time from SCUD launch to impact in the Gulf was about 7.5 minutes. In that time, a possible missile launch from Iraq had to be detected, processed, displayed, determined to be true, and then the fact of its launch and its azimuth and its projected range and target sent back into the theatre from NORAD. In order for theatre forces to take appropriate protective measures, they needed at least three or four minutes to react. So NORAD was working in a four-minute window.

NORAD Mission — Tomorrow?

As I approach the end of my allotted time, having touched the main geo-strategic factors and reviewed the history, mission and equipment, I should devote the remainder to the questions I posed earlier related to Canada and NMD and answer those with a "NORAD Tomorrow" perspective. Here are the questions, and my answers:

Should NMD become a NORAD mission and be tied into the Command, Control, Communications, Computers, Intelligence (C4I) structure? Yes it should. The main reasons are these: It is almost inconceivable that anytime soon the missions of aerospace warning and aerospace control (including air attack and defence) will become irrelevant to North American security. Indeed, the warning function already has applications beyond continental security interests and it would appear that those will only grow in the future. These essential capabilities are now entrenched in NORAD's mandate. Space-based infrared sensors, and ground-based missile detection radars that comprise the present missile attack warning system, when upgraded, will cue and direct the NMD kinetic kill interceptors. Because time is so critical and because the system is exclusively defensive in nature, it makes good sense to tie surveillance data and engagement data, and present that fused information to one commander.

Does the new mission fit in the structure at Cheyenne Mountain complex? Yes, it fits. The sharing of critical sensors was mentioned. Additionally, the physical infrastructure (Cheyenne Mountain) already exists; it is a sunk cost; needed communications architecture is in place or can be added; there is housing, life support, internal power; its location in the mountain is secure from saboteurs and terrorists. The alternative — the segregation of data that is fused together for sound tactical and technical reasons, solely to accommodate artificially divided mission responsibilities between partners — would be unwise militarily and would incur substantial costs. What are the technical risks? Who should pay?

Since inception, NORAD's mission of air defence has included detection, tracking, interception, and destruction of hostile aircraft penetrating North American airspace. That mission has endured even as strategy shifted from defence in the 1950s and 1960s, to deterrence in the 1970s and beyond. Nowadays there are new ballistic threats and, for the first time, technology to engage them, albeit in small numbers. A similar engagement sequence would take place — detect, track, intercept, & destroy. On what logic should one differentiate missions of aerospace warning and defence on the basis of delivery vehicle — be it air-breathing or be it ballistic? There is no such logic, and the differentiation should not be imposed. The missions both belong in one commander's terms of reference. It makes sense militarily and economically to combine the missions of warning and defence in one agency, under one commander.

What are the implications for Canada and NORAD if the US decides to deploy and Canada is not aboard? The issue is whether, in the new international circumstances, the interests of the two countries can be served better by NORAD or by new arrangements which are less integrated or less formal in character.

Given the things I have said about Canada in a dangerous world — its history of sharing continental defence, its status as a middle power bordering a superpower, it's traditional reluctance to spend money on defence, and the presence of a generous neighbor who may offer it free defence (or at *quid pro quo* rates) just for being a partner — all these things make the question hard for me to answer because I can't believe it would ever be asked. One might begin to construct a logical answer if one or other of the parties in this courtship would pop the question, so we knew what the conditions of the arrangement might be.

If I thought that NMD would genuinely perturb the new strategic relationship with Russia or other power, I perhaps could voice reservations about it. But I have none of those. The balance of nuclear power with our former adversary will, in my view, not be disturbed in any way by NMD in its planned configuration. Russian objections to NMD have, I think, been orchestrated and very clever political maneuvers, and not based on a legitimate strategic analysis of NMD's potential negative impact on stability, which is minuscule. If that allegation is correct, we should soon see amendments to ABM Treaty.

But the rogue state problem is dangerous and the consequence of our neglecting it could be horrific. It will become too plausible in the future to risk ignoring, and the accidental launch problem, unlikely as that may be, has been my worst nightmare for years. NMD will address both those risks.

Not to duck a direct question, I would add these comments. If NMD deployment proceeds and Canada is not on board, there will be a major disruption in the shared responsibility for continental defence. The integrated command structure would undergo radical change to segregate warning from engagement responsibilities. A Canadian could not be Deputy to the NORAD Commander-in-Chief because their terms of reference on mission responsibility would be so different. Canadians would be marginalized in the command structure, and probably excluded from upgraded missile warning sensors. Nor would they have access to newly sensitive work areas in Cheyenne Mountain, or to supporting commands and units. That's the bad news.

What connections exist between NMD and other Canada-US defence and security issues? Without participation, Canada's exposure to risk could increase significantly, as the US could quite reasonably locate the defensive system and tailor its engagement footprint strictly according to US interests. The surveillance and identification systems that support NMD will rely heavily on US space-based systems and Canada would not have either the information about what is going on in and over its own territory or the capability to obtain it. Both the exposure to risk and loss of surveillance information represent serious threats to and losses of Canadian sovereignty.

With participation, Canada's interests would be better served, while also reducing the risk to Canadians. It would also reinforce with our neighbors, responsible for over 85% of our trade, that we do want to contribute to continental security as well as to continue receiving benefits from a booming US economy. While such cross-sector linkages are normally discounted by responsible officials, they resonate with the man on the street in Richmond or Dallas who carries the short end of the defence stick, and wonders who his friends are.

Defence cooperation with the US over the last 60 years has not only contributed directly to Canadian and US security, but has also created the positive atmosphere that permits Canada to deal with the US on a host of other trans-border and international issues. Every Canadian has a stake in the outcome of these discussions and should, therefore, become familiar with the issues, the choices and the consequences of each, and be informed participants in the discussion. It is the least we can do for the security of our country and that of our partner to the south.

Conclusion

To finish on a positive note, a key point should be made: no single country, not even the remaining superpower, will be inclined to devote sufficient resources to possess all systems for all needs. Just as collaborative and cost-shared approaches to defence have worked in the past, so too can they work in the future. But first, we in Canada have to get the big things right and clearly understand what those things entail, and the consequences of each. Some of these big things are arms control-related. Some are defence and security related. All are important and need balance in a complicated security equation where the Canadian government's stance on NMD is unknown.

NATIONAL MISSILE DEFENCE AND THE FUTURE OF CANADA-US DEFENCE COOPERATION

Dr. Joseph T. Jockel

In the interest of time, and given my assignment, I will not be addressing the impact of a National Missile Defence (NMD) system on Canadian, US, or global security, but at the outset I'd also like to acknowledge that it is a central issue that needs to be assessed. Secondly, and also in the interest of time, I'm going to proceed from the assumption that the United States is going to deploy a National Missile Defence system. It is not a forgone conclusion, but it is highly likely at this moment. At any rate, for the purposes of what I'd like to look at, I'm not going to examine what will happen if the United States decides not to deploy an NMD system.

In thinking about Canada and NMD, I'm reminded of an old Stephen Leacock story, which you may have already heard. It's about an encounter between an American and a Canadian in the 1930s, the period right after the British 1931 Statute of Westminster gave Canada foreign policy autonomy, and before the outbreak of World War II. The American says to the Canadian, "If Britain goes to war, would you have to go to war?" The Canadian, very indignant, says "No!" So, the American says, "Well, if Britain goes to war, would you go to war?" The Canadian thinks for a moment and says, "Why, yes." The American says, "Why?" The Canadian says, "We'd have to."

That might be the outcome for the NMD debate in Canada. Canada does not have to participate in NMD. We should be very clear about that from the outset; neither Canadian territory, airspace or waters, nor the Canadian armed forces are necessary for the operation of the NMD sys-

---

Dr. Joseph T. Jockel is Professor of Canadian Studies at St. Lawrence University, Canton, NY.

tem. This is quite unlike the situation that faced our two countries in the 1950s when air defence was expanding outwards. In the early 1950s the Canadian cabinet was told, in essence, that it had no choice. The United States looked upon the establishment of new air defences as essential to the physical security of the United States. That is not what we're faced with. Both our countries really are free to choose whether or not to participate in NMD.

On the other hand, Canada may decide that it may have to participate in NMD because of NORAD. To put it in its simplest terms, without Canadian participation in NMD the North American Aerospace Defence Command has no future. To put it in slightly more sophisticated terms, without Canadian participation in NMD, you can have something that you can *call* NORAD (and which our two governments may very well call NORAD) but it won't *be* NORAD with its advantages and disadvantages to both of our countries. The critical issue is integrated tactical warning and assessment of nuclear attack on North America.

I'd like to put this very briefly into historical context. Back when NORAD was important, so was Canada, to the United States in terms of its defence. NORAD, at its inception, had operational command over all of North American air defences and, in Canada, that included no fewer than three great detection systems — the Distant Early Warning (DEW) Line, the Mid-Canada Line, and the Pine Tree Line — and no fewer than nine squadrons of RCAF aircraft. Later that included the famous Bomarc surface-to-air weapons The Bomarc and many of the aircraft were equipped with nuclear weapons. Canada was physically important to the security of the United States and undertook extensive aerospace defence operations.

NORAD's second task, in addition to air defence, was to provide warning, and later more sophisticated warning and assessment. Over the years, the importance of Canada to the United States declined, largely as a result of the shift from bombers to ballistic missiles. Today, the number of aircraft on standing alert in Canada for air defence purposes is four: two on the East Coast and two on the West Coast. The radar network is a shell, a peripheral system. At the same time, no system to detect or track ballistic missile has ever been located in Canada or operated by the Canadian Forces. As well, while Canada once had the capability to detect objects in orbit, that capability has now been lost with the closing of the Baker-Nunn cameras. In short, Canada's contribution to North American defence — aerospace defence — is now a very limited one of air defence.

And yet, Canadians sit at the very heart of the system in Colorado Springs, that heart being the Integrated Tactical Warning and Attack Assessment (ITWAA) process. Within Cheyenne Mountain, a joint Canada-US staff assess that fused data and a General or Flag officer, Canadian or American, takes turns being the assessor of whether or not there is an actual attack on North America. As long as Canadians are part of that process, which draws data from space surveillance operations and from missile detection and tracking operations, Canadians are at the very heart of NORAD.

The problem, from the point of view of Canada-US relations, is that the operational plan for national missile defence is to link the battle management of the system to the assessment of the system. In particular, the assessor will be given release authority over the National Missile Defence. That only makes sense. As General Morton underlined, it would only take several minutes for an attack on North America to occur — about four minutes — so it would make no sense to undertake the assessment, ask for its confirmation by a General or Flag officer, and then begin the process with a second set of officials. This is quite unlike the last US plans for missile defence, in which the (now defunct) Sprint system was deployed to defend nuclear missile bases and did not have the same political implications as National Missile Defence. The current US plan is to have a General officer, or Flag officer, have launch authority because under certain political circumstances it may make sense to not engage incoming missiles. So, in short, if there is no Canadian participation in National Missile Defence, there will be no Canadian participation in the future in ITWAA. The heart of NORAD will be gone. In the long run, if not in the short run, NORAD cannot survive. What then?

If NORAD Ends

Structurally, the end of NORAD would be easy to engineer. Arrangements have long existed whereby a US command (today it is US Space Command) could take over ITWAA. At NORAD's dissolution, should it come to that, the current U.S. Space Command could assume this responsibility permanently, although the US might take then the opportunity to reshuffle further its major command arrangements. Put more directly, NORAD is not essential to the United States — that is, NORAD being conceived as a joint Canada-US institution. Integrated tactical warning and assessment and other functions are still important, but the organization itself is not necessary to the United States.

Canada-US air defence cooperation would still be necessary. Conceivably, a small Canada-US air defence command could be created, which would also provide information to US Space Command or whichever US command had been given ITWAA. It might even continue to bear the NORAD name, in order to smooth over the rupture. But such an air defence command would hardly be necessary; the sorts of close Canada-US air defence cooperation which existed before 1957 without a joint command, would do. In short, the impact on US security of NORAD's dissolution is minimal, and you might extend that to Canada's security.

Since the US pays about 90 per cent of NORAD's costs, it might appear that its dissolution would oblige Canada to spend a lot of money to create and operate new command and control structures of its own. But this really would not be the case. In fact, for Canada there probably would be short-term budgetary savings arising from NORAD's demise, since Canada's role would be reduced to conducting air defence operations. For these, there already are adequate command and control facilities at the current 1 Canadian Air Division Headquarters located in Winnipeg (which now also is the headquarters of the Canadian NORAD Region), along with the underground Sector Air Operations Centre at North Bay, Ontario.

In fact, to stay in NORAD might actually cost the Canadian government some additional money. The US would not, in all probability, expect Canada to help pay for NMD, but it might well expect Canada to make what is being called by Canadian defence officials an "asymmetric contribution" to some other aspect of North American aerospace defence that the US might value. The Canadian military has also identified an area in which Canada might make such a new contribution: surveillance of space. Canada might become what a policy paper calls a "full partner" in the US Space Command's Space Surveillance Network, which tracks all objects in orbit around the earth. It serves several functions, not the least of which is warning of objects whose orbits have decayed, and which are about to enter the atmosphere. It can also be used to warn when spy satellites are overhead.

Space surveillance was once a Canadian specialty in NORAD until the 1980s, when new technology rendered obsolete the optical sensors located at Cold Lake Alberta and St. Margaret's, New Brunswick. The Canadian military hopes to reinvigorate this capability.[1]

Nonetheless, there could also be real, longer-term costs to Canada if the most important structure in the Canada-US defence relationship were dissolved (in essence if not in name), potentially beginning with limitations on Canada's future military capabilities. Space is increasingly important to the military. The Canadian Forces have a lengthy (and expensive) list of space capabilities they wish to acquire simply to support the army, navy, and air force in modern tactical environments. These include communications, navigation, search and rescue, intelligence, weather, and mapping projects. To achieve many of these, cooperation with the US military is key. As Professor Fergusson, from whom you heard this morning, argued in a comprehensive 1998 study of NMD commissioned by the Department of Foreign Affairs and International Trade, NORAD, especially because of its siamese-twin relationship to US Space Command, is critical for enhancing Canadian access to US military space projects and space-based assets. Thus, he concludes, if Ottawa declines to participate in NMD, "it is difficult to see how Canada could continue to participate in other key space-related activities in a joint way with the United States...In other words, Canada's future involvement in space may be at issue, with a wide range of possible political and budgetary implications..."[2]

There would also be some ripple effects into other areas of Canada-US relations, beyond the military sphere. At the very least, the bilateral defence economic relationship, recently so badly roiled over the ITAR issue, probably would become shakier as it became harder to justify special exemptions for Canadian firms, once Canada had left NORAD (or at had left the central portion of aerospace defence cooperation).

Canadian influence in Washington would decline. Great care has to be taken not to exaggerate here, for the influence argument has tended to be overstated since NORAD's very beginning and it has sometimes led to Canadian disappointment. As famously discovered by Prime Minister John Diefenbaker during the 1962 Cuban missile crisis, a scant five years after he agreed to NORAD's creation, the pledges made in the NORAD agreement for the two countries to consult can mean little in a true emergency. It would also be very difficult and probably impossible to identify any fundamental aspect of the US defence posture that, over the years, has been altered by Canada's exerting influence through NORAD.

With or without NORAD, Canada would, through NATO, be a member of the western alliance, with a seat at the table. Canada-US defence cooperation, including air defence cooperation, would also continue. We would still be partners. Still, it is hard to avoid the conclusion that if

NORAD were to go, Canada's long-term standing as a close ally whose views on matters of international security needed to be listened to and whose interests needed to be given most serious consideration would diminish, and not just with the US military, but also with the State Department, intelligence agencies, senior administration officials, and members of Congress. Washington might not be piqued or miffed at Canada, unless, of course Ottawa tried to lead a crusade to denounce NMD and the abrogation of the ABM Treaty. This is the worst-case scenario of Canada-US relations: an Axworthy crusade to denounce the US action. The two governments probably would work hard to smooth over any short-term symbolic damage the end of NORAD might cause. But over the years, Canada would just not count quite as much with the US government and so would not be viewed in quite the same fashion. After all, the United States would trust no other ally with the kind of responsibilities that General Morton had in Colorado Springs.

Canada's global standing could also be affected, although the same caution about exaggeration should be kept in mind. Some countries might be impressed with Canada's having loosened a security tie with the US. Others, especially those in NATO would not, knowing that Canada had lost the most important part of its special security relationship with the US, which had provided it with uniquely intimate access to and knowledge of the U.S. defence establishment.

Conclusion

The NMD issue might just not lead to differences between Washington and Ottawa after all, at least for the next several years. There certainly are plenty of possibilities: 1) Russia may at the last minute agree to an amendment to the ABM Treaty. This would free the Canadian government to swallow whatever doubts it may have about the necessity of deploying an NMD system to respond to North Korean, Iraqi and Iranian threats and also allow Ottawa to act to preserve NORAD; 2) the NMD tests scheduled for 2000 may fail, allowing the president to put off deployment, although in such a case, no one in Canada should think that US missile defence efforts will just go away; 3) President Clinton might decide that preserving the ABM treaty is more important than NMD, although here, too, the issue will, under Republican pressure, not go away. (And since, in many senses, the real purpose of NMD is to protect Al Gore from Republicans and not protect the United States from missile threats, I don't think that is a likely decision!); 4) finally, Canadians and their government might even come to agree with the US administration that since NMD does not threaten the intent of the ABM Treaty, it is not reasonable to give Russia a veto over actions needed for the defence of the US. They might even come to the conclusion that defending North America against missile attacks by countries such as North Korean, Iran and Iraq is not such a bad idea.

In recent years, we have grown steadily used to the increasing integration of Canada and the US, especially in the economic relationship. For purposes of defence, though, geography no longer ties Canada and the US quite as closely together as in the past — at least for aerospace defence (although some homeland defence issues are quite different). In the case of NORAD, a measure of institutional disintegration is conceivable. If the outcome over the coming year or so is 5) abrogation of the ABM Treaty and deployment of the NMD over the continuing objections of not just Russia but of Canada, the Canada-US relationship will be strained. Perhaps then some satisfaction is to be had for both Canadians and Americans in that both our countries will be free to choose on this matter, each according to its priorities.

Notes

1. Canada, Department of National Defence, Directorate of Space Development, "A Canadian Military Space Strategy," 21 April 1998.

2. James Fergusson, "Canada and Ballistic Missile Defence: Issues, Implications, and Timelines," Non-proliferation, Arms Control and Disarmament Division, Department of Foreign Affairs and International Trade, Ottawa, 1998, 70.

AFTERNOON FORUM

Jeffrey Simpson, *The Globe and Mail*

Frances Fitzgerald, the author of *Fire in the Lake* about Vietnam, has just written a book. I haven't read it yet (it's just out) but I've read two reviews of it. She reminds us that the previous and much larger Strategic Defense Initiative (SDI) cost some 60 billion dollars and was operationally deemed not to be functional. From what I have been reading, following this issue in the *New York Times* and the *Wall Street Journal*, the success rate of the American military in its prescribed efforts has been something that if it were a baseball hitter would probably consign it to the A leagues rather than the major leagues. We haven't actually talked about how successful these tests have been. Can you give us an update, General, on this? Has anybody hit anything yet? There has been one quasi success — there's a long William Broad story in the *New York Times* about how the Pentagon had camouflaged the failures of previous tests.

LGen (Retd) Robert W. Morton

There has been one kinetic kill — a direct impact. Even in a near miss with all of the observation mechanisms that are being used, there are things to be derived in a positive sense from a near miss. I really can't get too excited about the test failures that have occurred thusfar. When you've been in the back end of an AWACS or in the cockpit of a CF-18 and you've gone through an evolution of 35 years of technical equipment in that period, you realize that if you put your mind and your money to it, you're going to be able to do whatever it is you want to do in this era. Just to make the point, you're aware of the Phalanx close-in defence system that our navy has. In the days of the prototype development of the Phalanx (Hughes Aircraft Company was working on it) they fired a five-inch navy shell toward a ship on which a Phalanx was located. I saw that

---

The session was chaired by Jeffrey Simpson, columnist with *The Globe and Mail*.

five-inch shell sitting on a desk in California and it had six pockmarks in it. When that shell entered into the engagement envelope of the Phalanx it was struck six times by 20 mm rounds before it hit the water and was recovered. So, I totally reject the notion of 'it ain't technically possible'.

Mr. Simpson

Dr. Jockel, is that what you meant when you were telling us that even if the tests failed this year, don't be misled, the pressure for this is going to continue and at some point the political and military circumstances will come together and there will be some form of a system, even if all the tests are failing now.

Dr. Joseph T. Jockel

Yes. The timetable for the tests is set by politics, not by technology. I don't think that anyone, even the most fervent supporters of NMD, would claim that by this June when the president is scheduled to make his decision a complete picture is going to be in front of them. That's why I think the point that Mr. Robinson made is important — that there's going to be a decision in June and there's going to be a decision the year after. There will be an endless series of decisions.

Mr. Simpson

This will be my last moderator's prerogative. From Canada's point of view could you argue à la John A MacDonald that all tomorrow's strategy isn't bad? In other words, if there's a failure this summer and there's an agreement by the president dictated by political reasons, the real operational decisions won't be made until further down the road when more successes that have so far eluded the US military might be in hand.

Dr. Jockel

No. Within a year of a decision to go, it is highly likely that the United States will then tender a formal invitation to Canada to participate. At that point, some hard decisions will have to be made in Ottawa. I think the Chretien government has been doing it exactly right up until now. There is no reason to reach any kind of decision now. You are right about June, but about a year thereafter things could change.

Dr. George Lindsey, former Director of Operational Research, DND

We've been given some rather good answers about whether this thing is going to work, and also some other ideas about whether Canada needs to make up its mind in a hurry. I've seen military things go through periods of as much as 20 years of research and development. And when it's as complicated as this you have to expect test failures, rewrites, years and years go by, and this is probably the most complicated thing that has ever been devised by military people. The idea that three tests are going to tell you whether it's going to work is just crazy. I think it's surprising that they scheduled only 19 tests, but to make up their mind after three, they might as well just close their eyes and stick a pin in a pig's eye or something like that.

Odds are that test number three will miss, but that shouldn't stop them from going ahead eventually. But there's such a difference between scheduling a research and development (R&D) program and putting all your resources into it and doing it well, and making the decision for deployment. Deployment is where the real money begins to pile up and I would have thought that the sensible thing for the Americans to do would be to go on with their R&D and then every year say "Well, should we go on with R&D for another year?" I don't see why 2000 has to be the deadline for them to decide to deploy NMD. What's the big hurry?

LGen (Retd) Morton

If you look at the current national intelligence estimates and views in the United States from the Rumsfeld Commission and elsewhere, the general view is that rogue states, particularly North Korea, could acquire ICBM capability much quicker [than anticipated]. Perhaps within two to three years. I think the general view from a lot of people I've talked to is that they're looking at 2004, 2005, 2006 as the most likely date of operational capability. The hurry then becomes, according to the planners, that if the United States does not make a decision this year, then it cannot start pouring concrete next summer in Alaska and you need to pour concrete next summer in order to have an operational NMD capability by 2005. And every year you delay puts off an operational capability for another year, and that's why, at least from the planner's side, there is pressures for a decision this year.

Dr. Jockel

How quickly Canada might act could depend upon the ultimate intensity of the government of Canada's arms control convictions. That is, if the United States starts heading down a path that leads to abrogation of the ABM treaty, and if the government of Canada decides that its arms control principles are more important than some of these other concerns that we've talked about, or the impact would be so deleterious on the arms control regime, it might decide to take an earlier decision, to step in somehow to encourage the United States not to proceed. I'm not sure how, but that could precipitate an earlier decision.

Mr. Simpson

But what's your response to Dr. Lindsey's question, which is, I think, what's the rush? The answer [from General Morton] was "the North Koreans are coming, the Koreans are coming." Is that your answer as well?

Dr. Jockel

Well, the Rumsfeld Commission does point to the development of that capability by them. You can't deny that there is politics involved. There's an election this November, NMD in the current phase is fairly popular in the United States, there's a president who never saw a popular issue he didn't want to co-opt, and all of these things have come together to create much more a political than a technical timetable.

Dave Hanley, *Ottawa Citizen*

Two questions. In the spirit of the event, I've come here officially representing the Ottawa Citizen, and unofficially as someone who is going to go back potentially to these rogue states and their question to me, which I ask you, is, "If we put 20 missiles towards you and one gets through, a failsafe sort of scenario, what is your reaction going to be to us in Iraq or us in North Korea? Are you going to respond in kind, as you probably would have with the Russians, times ten say, and risk fallout over Israel if you hit Iraq or over South Korea if you hit North Korea?" In other words, what is the exit strategy that's beyond NMD once it's in place, and assuming it's needed, and assuming that potentially it fails? What is the US reaction to a country sending missiles its way? I'm just wondering if that changes any strategic thinking.

LGen (Retd) Morton

As a former operative in the Integrated Tactical Warning and Attack Assessment (ITWAA), your question really is totally outside my area of responsibility or experience. That is probably the same answer you'd get from any Canadian military officer, and I doubt that there are very many US military officers either who ever have access to the matrix of options that might be presented by the secretary of defense to the president, in consultation with other advisors, as to what his response is going to be. In other words, it's not a forgone conclusion that the response will be of one magnitude or another. My thinking about NMD is that it allows the introduction of a diplomatic option. It allows the engagement of small numbers of rogue or mistaken launches toward the United States.

Every military system that's ever been designed ends up with a probability of kill. So, if you were to buy a system that the manufacturer would warranty to a 0.95 probability of success, you're getting a pretty good system. Most military systems operate in a 0.85 to 0.95 range. Every weapons systems that you build has a CEP, a circular error of probability. They don't land exactly where they are aimed. That's why I made the point about a little variation in azimuth or direction; if it is really aimed at Buffalo and doesn't burn for the right number of seconds, it lands in Toronto instead. We're caught in this by virtue of our geography. So, no one other than the President of the United States can answer your question. I'm suggesting to you that the introduction of a means of defending yourself from a mistaken or intentional small attack introduces a brand new dimension to the whole business of diplomacy and international relationships. If the military can say to the president, we can stop this, or stop most of these, the president immediately has a new line on his matrix of options. So I don't see a tit-for-tat response to a rogue country with the NMD program. To me, that is a very positive addition to the arsenal of the United States and the world.

Bill Robinson

Well, I would disagree with that. I think that even if the defence were successful and it stopped missiles from coming in — I'm talking about an intentional launch now — that there's no way that the US would sit back and apply a diplomatic approach. What you're talking about here is a country that has just launched weapons of mass destruction at the United States, which, through luck, the United States was capable of intercepting. The hostile country has the intent to deliver such weapons, it presumably has not exhausted its arsenal and could try again and might get through the next time. The idea that they're going to send Strobe Talbott to Pyongyang to give them a nasty letter is just untenable. The US would be falling back on the threat of retaliation. Although it would probably be nuclear, it would not necessarily be, as the US is quite capable of removing the regime in Pyongyang with conventional means if it chose to expend the lives necessary to do so, but you would definitely be talking about responses on that level. The idea that a lucky intercept would cause them not to respond I think is beyond credibility.

Mr. Hanley

My second question follows that directly. Is it possible that it is not so much Russia or China's deterrent forces that would be diminished, or in their eyes diminished, but America's? I base that question on what I see as potentially one of the fundamental flaws of this defence system: it's not so much the insecurity it may create either because of bickering with allies or new relationships with the Chinese or the Russians or the technology itself. It's not the insecurity it creates, but perhaps the insecurity it projects if the rogue states perceive that there's an absolute terror of Seattle being hit or New York being hit. Of course we were terrified that the Russians were going to hit us as well, but now it's not so much to project through MAD a whole range of retaliatory forces, but rather to defend ourselves. As soon as that insecurity is projected, does that not remove our deterrent capability if they think that we will not necessarily retaliate? Because we are projecting fear — and fear in the eyes of the opponent is a huge advantage, even when you're the weaker side — are we not projecting a measure of our own terror? We are doing a responsible thing, I imagine, in wanting to defend ourselves, but because of that projection of insecurity, we are putting into their minds a sense that these people, as they flew at 15,000 feet in Kosovo, don't want to see any bodybags, in any circumstance, and therefore they're terrified of being hit and maybe they're not so keen about retaliating.

Dr. Jockel

Briefly, about your first question. It seems to me that you've underlined the weakness of the argument of deterrence and the argument for defence, because you can extend your question. What if more missiles had gotten through? Is the only policy option that the President of the United States to have is to burn 10 million people to death? Is that the kind of response that he has to contemplate under those circumstances? By putting a defensive system in place, you remove (if it works) that kind of choice having to be made.

Your second question. Well, yes definitely. Who would not be worried and frightened about North Koreans or others acquiring nuclear weapons to strike at the United States? Such a threat does not exist now and who would not be worried about it? Particularly, imagine a North Korean attack on South Korea, imagine an Iraqi attack on Kuwait with no defence system, in which the North Koreans say "we can kill hundreds of thousands or millions of Americans. Your only response if we do that will be to burn to death 20 million of our people." I think under those circumstance the President of the United States would pause seriously before authorizing intervention in those conflicts.

Peggy Mason, Canadian Council for International Peace and Security (CCIPS)

All the speakers have acknowledged the importance of the global security implications of the deployment of a National Missile Defence system. So I guess what I'd like to do is ask the question to each of the speakers: if they put themselves in the position of a Chinese defence planner, given the limited nature of the strategic nuclear deterrent that China has, what would *you* be recommending to the Chinese leadership in response to the US deployment of an alleged limited National Missile Defence in circumstances where either the US has abrogated the ABM treaty or, even if they reached a decision with the Russians to allow for limited deployment, you have a Senate that is adamantly opposed to any restrictions on the deployment. So in those circumstances, do you as a defence planner say "well, we have to trust in the American administration, they say it's going to be limited." And even there, even if it was limited, given the limited nature of the Chinese nuclear deterrent, what do you as a defence planner tell your leadership to do in response.

LGen (Retd) Morton

I've never projected myself into advising Peking on military matters. My sense is that Chinese military policies are more wrapped up in their regional concerns than they are focused on US concerns. I don't think that the National Missile Defence deployment decision will have one iota of effect in changing what China has set a course to achieve. China has a deployed ICBM system now, they're working on submarine-launched ballistic missiles, they're improving their aircraft systems, and presumably their nuclear arsenal will continue to grow. So, while there is a lot of rhetoric about it, I don't think that China's interests really enter into the equation of National Missile Defence decision-making in this country. If I were a Chinese air force general, how would I advise? This is really not my responsibility until I get asked the question by the political leadership in China. Certainly my enthusiasm for world and regional stability would result in my advising my political leadership on what I think is required based upon the threat that is either in existence or appearing on the horizon. There is no direct military threat from the United States to China.

Dr. Jockel

My advice would be simple: close down all the missiles. The United States is not a threat to the physical security of China, China has no need of intercontinental ballistic missiles in its defence relationship with the United States.

Mr. Robinson

Well, I advise them all to shut down their missiles but they don't listen to me. The Chinese are going to insist on keeping their capability just the same as the United States and Russia do. As I mentioned in my talk, Beijing does feel the need to deter the United States — particularly US intervention in Chinese regional issues. They feel the need for that capability and they will act to preserve it. I think that's inevitable and it's what any general in Beijing would recommend.

Dr. Jockel

I think that's what's going to happen as well if the US deploys. My advice will not be taken and in all probability there will be an expansion in the number of Chinese missiles. But that may be in the cards anyway. Remember, ten or fifteen years ago the Chinese stole the plans for miniaturized warheads from the United States and may be planning a significant increase in their missile inventory and could continue that beyond the level needed to penetrate the National Missile Defence which, as I'm sure was talked about earlier, would in its first phase be able to destroy incoming missiles (if it works) in the low tens, and in the second phase in the higher tens.

LGen (Retd) Morton

Could I add a comment about Peggy's question? Because of the horrific nature of the subject, a lot of the questions in seminars like this tend to assume that these things, once they're built and deployed, are really going to be used. And yet the purpose of every offensive and defensive system since the dawn of the nuclear age, after the Second World War ended, has been 'what do you do to prevent these systems from being used'. The whole notion of nuclear weapons bringing into existence a condition in which the weapons that are deployed must never be used is the trigger that drives all of the operational analysis that leads to the production of different kinds of systems. So my presumption about National Missile Defence is that you think through the strategy, you consider the ideology and motivators of the people you're concerned about, you look at their technological capability and you build something that will prevent them from taking the action that you fear. That is the nature of defensive activity in all of my 37 years of military experience.

Mr. Simpson

Can I ask a follow up to that? In all areas of planning there is a kind of cost-benefit analysis; a risk-probability analysis. Reference has been made twice to the Rumsfeld report. There was a very vigorous and high profile riposte to that report by people from the security elements of the United States, which said that the report had substantially overestimated the threat. So I, as a layperson, am left with two reports that contradict each other. I'm left also looking at one of the poorest countries in the world — North Korea — that can't even feed its own people and I see people in Washington waxing very rhetorically about the threat it poses. How much of this rhetoric is being driven by people who've been working on some variation of anti-ballistic missile defence for many years now and don't want to let it go, ie. the contractors, the people who are getting rich off this, the politicians whose districts are getting the contracts, whose voters are employed? How much of this is just kind of the inertia? Cain said we are all ruled by old ideas. How much of it is that, and how much of it is a real, considered threat that the North Koreans, within a reasonable period of time, not being able to feed their own people, are going to amass a sufficient number of weapons to seriously threaten San Francisco?

LGen (Retd) Morton

There are no answers to those questions that I could volunteer that would satisfy you. Jim Fergusson may have some answers about Rumsfeld and rebuttals to it. The capabilities-intention dilemma is a variation in motivators that I have detected in my many years of duty with US military officers, and I call it the December 7 syndrome. I think that, having been struck once, caught napping and suffering a serious military defeat, even a temporary one, has motivated the US military in its advice to its political leadership to focus on the capability and make sure you can do something about that capability and not ignore, but put in a subservient place, the whole issue of intention. And so, if you have a space launch vehicle, a three stage vehicle, and there is indication that there is research and development to improve the throw weight and the range and therefore strike targets further away or launch heavier loads into space, then the motivation south of the border is going to be 'do something about it'. The motivation on our side of the border is often 'yes, but would they do it?'. So there is an interesting dichotomy of view on how quickly one should react to what is perceived to be a capability, regardless of what the intentions might appear to be. The Americans react to capability.

Mr. Robinson

I think there are a variety of reasons why the American are pursuing this. There is the domestic political one; the Clinton administration sees it purely in that lens, I think. There are the missile defence zealots, there are institutional interests in the space command, for example, and there are, of course, industrial interests that lead them to blow up a potential technological capability into a major threat. And by far the best explanation of what the North Koreans are up to is almost certainly that they're manipulating that capability as a way of buying outside aid and economic engagement with the outside world. It's already their source of hard currency but potentially it's a way for them to improve regime survival.

One thing on the capabilities and intentions, just briefly. It is ironic that they focus entirely on capabilities when it comes to those so-called threats, because they are asking the Russians and the Chinese to focus purely on intentions when it comes to what the United States is doing. The United States' capability, offensive and defensive put together as potential breakout is extremely frightening, if you assume even the possibility of bad intentions. You have to assume purely good intentions on the part of the United States — they are asking the world to do that — at the same time as they do not look at all at that on their side.

Dr. Jim Fergusson

I have a comment following what General Morton said and then I have a question from what Bill just said, which I'd be very interested in his response to. I think there's a great degree of misunderstanding of what the recommendation or the argument of the Rumsfeld Commission was. The fundamental argument that's been made public — and I think it was expressed through the executive summary — simply says that the former 1995 national intelligence estimate, which put the probability of a capability among rogue states down the road ten to fifteen years, may be wrong. There is a chance that these states may acquire these capabilities quicker than we think. However, the key argument that the Commission made was that there could readily be an intelligence failure where they would acquire them and we wouldn't know about it. And what made the Rumsfeld commission report so viable politically in the United States was that it was shortly followed by the North Korean test, which the intelligence failed to know was coming, then by the Indian nuclear detonations, which the intelligence community also failed on, then to a less degree Pakistan's nuclear tests.

That is the heart of their argument; if they're going down this path, why not invest now and deploy defences so that they are in place, rather than wait until the rogue states have the capability? I think that it is also important that we not forget that the three main rogue threats that the Americans talk about — North Korea, Iraq and Iran — are all in areas where there are either forward-deployed American forces (there is, after all, a treaty commitment in South Korea) or major strategic interests like the one that the United States went to war over in 1990-91. There's a political element to this involving a simple question: will the President of the United States be able to stand in front of the American public and say "I can deploy missile defences for my forces in the field, but I can't protect my own people at home." And I think that's an important part of the political equation.

Now, after that, then my question to Mr. Robinson. I agree entirely with your assessment on North Korea, that they have used the threat of nuclear weapons, by the threat to withdraw from the NPT, as political blackmail, and they have used the test of the three-stage missile and the whole missile issue as political blackmail. Why then isn't developing missile defences good for western political strategy in removing that political card from that totalitarian regime, so we don't have to bend to that regime?

Mr. Robinson

The simple answer to that is that you're perturbing nations that are a lot more important to our safety — namely Russia and China. So if you're going to shoot your brains out in order to threaten North Korea, you know it's not a smart move. On the Rumsfeld Commission, I agree that it has been misinterpreted a lot. One of the things that's been misinterpreted about it is that it called for missile defence, which it didn't. It talked purely about technological capabilities, including the possibility that you could get somebody to sell it to you. So, any country in the world has the technological capability in five years to have a ballistic missile, if they buy it from somebody who's already built one. And that's basically that. It did not say that it was a good idea to make missile defences. In fact, Richard Garwin, who was a participant in the panel, is a strong opponent of missile defences for the sort of reasons that I talked about. On the question of the intervention, I think that's a problem the United States is going to have to accept. If it sets invulnerability as a pre-condition for intervention, it might as well get out of the business, because you cannot protect a country against weapons of mass destruction with all the various means of delivery that can be developed. If they want to be able to intervene against countries like that, they're going to have to run the risk.

CLOSING REMARKS

BGen (Retd) W. Don Macnamara

Ladies and gentlemen, it's been a fun-filled day with lots of discussion and lots of new, and reinterpretation of old, information. Before I get into the formal summation, I'd just like to say that as a former sometime-strategic planner, 'capabilities and intentions' was the kind of argument that used to drive us crazy because there are another two sides to the square. The other two sides are incentives and opportunities. So if you are really going to do an analysis of the strategic equation, you've got to take capabilities, intentions, incentives and opportunities all into account, and make sure that you either don't let your opponent fill in the square, or make sure that you have the square filled in ahead of him. On that note, I'd like to move on to the formal summation, and you will be pleased to learn that it is not my intention to regurgitate all the remarks that have been delivered to us today except to say that we have had a very good and very rich experience.

We started off this morning with regional discussions by Drs. Robert Henderson and Jim Fergusson, who gave us some insights into those things that we don't necessarily see and hear and, for that matter, discuss amongst ourselves. Dr. Henderson examined some of the things that are going on in Asia and how they relate, both intra-Asia and in the context of our relations and those of the United States, with that region. It was very useful to be able to talk about the sensitivities and issues confronting Japan, Taiwan, and Korea. The continuing discussion of China throughout the day was also particularly interesting.

Dr. Fergusson did us a great service in trying to clarify the European dimensions of NMD, which we have heard and read about so little in our national media. Clearly, these stories may bear some serious re-

---

BGen (Retd) W. Don Macnamara is Past President of the CISS.

interpretation and discussion of their accuracy. Particularly interesting was his discussion of the American position, European concerns about disengagement of the US from Europe, and his recognition that there are two things the Europeans want to do: avoid the US disengagement on the one hand, but at the same time be able to integrate their systems on the other.

We were then particularly privileged to have the Minister of National Defence find time in his schedule to come and address us this morning. I found it very interesting that he was able to — I wouldn't say walk a tightrope — but he did a very good job laying out the various components of the strategic issues and the political issues, and the kinds of discussions that are going to have to take place not just in Cabinet, not just within the government, but broadly across the population. When David Rudd made his introductory remarks, he said that it was the aim of our seminar to develop a more informed discussion of these issues on the part of all Canadians. I think the Minister pointed that out this morning, how important it is that we have an informed discussion, and as broad as possible discussion, with the Canadian population.

This afternoon (and because it is relatively recent, I won't reiterate all of the components) Bill Robinson brought up a number of issues that we have to take into account — either confirm or refute — in terms of the case against ballistic missile defence. He was followed by Bob Morton who made some compelling arguments on the other side of the equation, particularly the issue of Canadian sovereignty. Dr. Joseph Jockel's discussion in the final analysis left us with this rather interesting conundrum: we don't have to be part of it but perhaps we must. That is another major issue that we have to take into account.

However, I think that it's also interesting and useful to remember that this morning, during the question period, Dr. Henderson made reference to the statement that 'money and technology cannot remake geography.' If I'm going to leave here today with anything ringing in my head, it is going to be that idea, along with the other comment by Dr. Jockel, that 'we may not have to, but maybe we must.' Those two statements are things that I'm going to have to think about now and in the future.

That just leaves me to thank, on your behalf, all of our speakers, this morning and this afternoon, our moderators this morning and this afternoon, Executive Director David Rudd and Jim Hanson who organized and planned this activity, and Research Officer Jessica Blitt and her volunteer staff who made today possible. We recognize that this is not necessarily the best accommodation in Ottawa but we will respond to that on another occasion. It has been a very fruitful time to have all of you here. As well as thanking all those people who put this on, I'd also like to thank all of you for being here, because without you it wouldn't have been half the seminar it has been.